2016
YOUR BEST YEAR

PRODUCTIVITY WORKBOOK &
CREATIVE BUSINESS PLANNER

by Lisa Jacobs

YOUR BEST YEAR 2016 BY LISA JACOBS

TABLE OF CONTENTS

HOW TO USE THIS PLANNER	3
INTRODUCTION	8
SECTION 1: REVIEW	10
END-YEAR REFLECTIONS AND REVIEW	11
NEW YEAR POLICIES AND PLANNING	16
IF I KNEW I COULD NOT FAIL	22
THE POWER OF 3'S	26
PRIORITIZE YOUR BIG IDEAS	36
SECTION 2: PREPARE	39
MAKE IT HAPPEN ALREADY	40
THE SECRET TO SUCCESS	41
A VOW FOR 2016	48
NEW HABITS FOR A NEW YOU	49
SCHEDULE PROGRESS REVIEWS	52
SECTION 3: DO	53
YOUR ITINERARY FOR 2016	54
2016 TABLE OF CONTENTS	56
PROGRESS LOGS	59, 79, 105, 125
MID-YEAR REVIEW	98
TIPS TO STAY ON TRACK	144

© 2015-2016 Lisa Jacobs
All rights reserved

HOW TO USE THIS PLANNER

This workbook is filled to the brim with best year-making prompts, goal-setting exercises, and review sections. I'm in the mood for big changes, and I hope you are, too!

If I hear one more person downplay the importance of New Year resolutions, I'm going to scream! Not because I'm a huge believer of resolutions (I don't even set them), but because it allows people to settle back into their comfort zones so they can keep doing the same things, all the while expecting different results! The fact of the matter is:

> **HIGH-PERFORMING PEOPLE SET GOALS RELIGIOUSLY AND TRACK THEM RELIGIOUSLY. THEY OBSESS ABOUT WHETHER THEY'RE HITTING OR MISSING THOSE GOALS, AND WHY.**
>
> **IF YOU DON'T SET AND TRACK GOALS, LIFE JUST PASSES YOU BY.**
> — *Cameron Herold*

And that's my goal for *Your Best Year*: to help you become a high-performing person who refuses to allow life to pass you by.

You see, it dawned on me a while back that we're all running our businesses day-by-day (including me), and if you reflect on that for a moment, you'll realize how disturbing it is. We're the only small business owners *in the world* who try to operate, let alone succeed this way!

A serious business person doesn't scramble, she schedules. A real businesswoman doesn't try something one day, check stats, and give up! No, she persists. She continues to pursue her goals.

So, I spent 2015 observing thriving small businesses and asking myself:

What do they know that we don't?

What I learned is this: A thriving entrepreneurship is based on seasons, and we're failing to appreciate and utilize its natural rhythm.

For example, one of my clients came out of a phenomenal holiday season; her sales were off-the-chart from both show and online. About two weeks later, she wrote me an email to tell me that now everything she's doing is "resulting in crickets." She's clearing flying by the seat of her pants; riding high during busy season and crash-landing as soon as it ends.

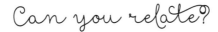

Let's look at it another way: Her business is doing fine, but she's failing to *appreciate* and *utilize* its seasons. Are you with me? This isn't about what happened last month or what online campaign didn't produce the results that you anticipated yesterday.

It is about understanding the peaks and crests of your business so that you can plan and persist accordingly. This book is designed to help you do just that.

A FEW THINGS YOU MIGHT LIKE TO GATHER BEFORE YOU GET STARTED:

#1 At least one day planner

I run a multi-faceted creative business and two day planners help me separate the plans and goals I create. I keep a day planner for my blog (it serves as an editorial calendar and note-keeper) and another one that oversees my entire operation and schedule. I'll explain this in more detail later in the series, but in the last section, I'm going to issue important tasks for you to plug into your day planner in order to keep you on track.

#2 A giant drawing pad

While you're in the paper section picking out your day planner, pick up a children's giant drawing pad also. They're typically 16×22", and they are great for mapping out big projects and goals. You can find them in the Crayola aisle.

 *Things you need (cont'd)*

 ### #3 Alone time

I choose to do my annual review and intention-setting when I can find some solitude, over a period of about four days. I typically spend one to two hours in reflection, and I set the mood so that it is gentle, calm and sober. If that's not possible for you, carve out a block of quiet time in one day (give yourself at least three hours).

I'll take no excuses here: make this alone time happen. I'm a married mother of four, and I'm determined to honor this sacred practice. I'll go to my bedroom and send the "do not disturb" message before I begin. Self-reflection is critical to your wellbeing. Once you start a session, you are not to be interrupted.

#4 Space to spread out

I prefer the living room floor, but any wide-open space will do. It's always better to do planning + review exercises outside of your normal work space; it allows for fresh perspective and new ideas.

 ### #5 Comfort items

Be sure to have ready a delicious ice water and/or hot drink, favorite pens, and any additional resources you plan on using. If possible, turn off electronic distractions.

 ### #6 Pen and paper

Be sure to write down *everything* that occurs to you. If you stop to think about something as you reflect, record it.

When you follow the rumination of the mind *without* pen and paper, you chase thoughts that are too scattered to truly connect. Writing down any new ideas, problems, uncomfortable feelings, etc., lets them escape to the page where they can be reworked and shaped into successful projects or changes.

GET YOUR MIND RIGHT

The next thing you'll need to do to get the most out of this workbook and planner is to get your mind right. In this book, we're going to talk about how demanding a creative career can be, how difficult it is to persist when you're not getting the sales you desperately need, and how deflating it is to not receive the recognition you regularly crave.

This business is no joke.

In fact, this job is hard work, and it's ridden with obstacles and problems. Even worse and as you advance, there's less and less advice out there on how to build the career of your dreams. Because that's the thing: *It's so uniquely yours.*

As a consultant, I find too many creative business owners feeling stuck and trapped by their problems in business. We sometimes get very comfortable with our obstacles, for one reason or another:

- We like the nurturing attention it brings from the outside world;
- We're addicted to the dramatics an unsolved problem adds to our life; or
- **Most likely, we feel overwhelmed, uncertain and too scared to take the first step in the right direction.**

Nothing upsets me more than when I catch myself keeping problems, and I set out to remedy them as soon as I realize I'm being held hostage by an obstacle.

You're worth much more than your problems.

And I'm here to tell you that solving your own issues is the secret to your success. Alleviate your own complaints. Don't know how? Learn. Look at the individual obstacle for what it is, whether it be growing an email list, gaining more sales, finding paying customers, or mastering social media. Somebody's done it before, and you can do it too.

I look around at my peers, my partners and my affiliates, and I realize that the one thing we all have in common is this: *we stuck with it*. We kept building. When we were faced with an issue, we too complained, but then we examined the obstacle and hurdled it.

HURDLE YOUR OBSTACLES

How do you get from where you are to where you want to be? You physically move toward it; you take the actions necessary to get you there. If you wanted to travel from Pittsburgh to New York, you can't sit down on a park bench in Pittsburgh and wonder why you're not getting to New York.

It seems too simple to be true, but few people actively take action toward their goals. Most people are sitting on a park bench in Pittsburgh complaining about how their dreams aren't showing up for them. Can New York show up in Pittsburgh? No!

Your Best Year is here.

This book is a monster, hungry for your obstacles and starved for your achievement. Are you ready to feed it?

In section one, you're going to explore the past year to both appreciate how far you've come *and* face the obstacles that have been blocking your path. You'll then set up some policies and game-changers for the year ahead and get your first look at a new goal-setting system I designed to help you make it happen *already* in 2016.

In section two, you'll enjoy exercises and inspiration to help you prepare for the exciting progress you're going to make this year.

In section three, you'll find a complete system designed to help you accomplish whatever goals you set for yourself this year.

INTRODUCTION

Welcome to *Your Best Year: 2016 Productivity Workbook and Creative Business Planner!* This is the third annual edition of this project, and it's my favorite thing to create every year because I love self-discovery, progress, results and growth. And because I love it so, I'm absolutely honored to be on your journey as well!

But first, let's cover the hard parts. One of the most difficult aspects of creative business is the uncertainty and lack of validation.

A creative career is demanding.

Yes, I'm typing to you in my pajamas under a blanket on my couch with a steamy cup of decaf vanilla chai beside me. The irony is not lost on me. But, I'll say it again: a creative career is demanding.

I make it all up as I go along! I don't know where next month's paycheck is going to come from; I'll figure it out next month. I don't know what's going to sell or what's going to fail. I don't know if I'll get paid for the forty hours I've already invested into my next project. It could be all for naught.

I'll bet you can relate, and that's exactly why *Your Best Year* exists for creative entrepreneurs. It's here to be your motivator and personal assistant, your navigational guide, and the keeper of your vision.

Your Best Year is designed to help you create the results you desire and make it happen *already* in 2016. After coaching hundreds of creatives individually, I've learned one thing for sure: people need to be repeatedly reminded of their goals and reinforced in their efforts in order to progress.

If you're anything like I was, you're showing up year after year in business, doing the same things and expecting different results. Let me save you the five years it took me to learn this lesson: That strategy just doesn't work! In fact, there have been multiple times I've wanted to quit. But then I thought,

What if my career were different?

In case we're just meeting for the first time (as *Your Best Year* tends to take on a life of its own), I'm Lisa Jacobs. I'm a creative business owner and consultant, and I write the blog, Marketing Creativity.[1]

For years, I was doing what I call the "daily scramble" in business. And sadly, this is how the majority of creative business owners operate. The daily scramble means you wake up *today* and ask yourself: *What am I going to do today to get some sales already?* And the scramble begins!

> "Why, I'll send an email! I'll promote this post on Facebook! I'll make four new products and list them in the shop, and then I'll tweet each of them so everyone will come check them out!"

Instead of doing the daily scramble, imagine knowing where your next month's paycheck is coming from and feeling confident about how much you can earn. Imagine a set-it and forget-it system that builds your following, increases your sales, and markets your products while you sleep. Imagine having a realistic plan you can trust for constant expansion and growth.

When I set out on the challenge to build that dream for myself, I didn't know how to achieve it. But, I was willing to experiment. In 2014, I lived a year of full disclosure; I tallied my hours, tracked my progress and shared my income reports.

Then, in January of 2015, I doubled my average month's income from the previous year. I started February knowing that on the 28th of the month, I'd receive a guaranteed paycheck worth thousands for services already rendered. I had the whole month to earn *more* money, and I could sleep easy knowing that, no matter what, my minimum budget had been met. Imagine that!

In building a profitable creative business, you must give up waiting for things to happen and always be making your next purposeful move. Essentially, that means giving up scrambling for planning and persistence.

I'm here to help you make that happen.

---

[1] WWW.MARKETYOURCREATIVITY.COM

SECTION 1
REVIEW

YOUR BEST YEAR 2016

by Lisa Jacobs

END-YEAR REFLECTIONS AND REVIEW

We are going to kick off *Your Best Year* by reviewing the past year. It's important to review, reflect upon, learn from and appreciate all that happened in 2015 in order to achieve the results you want in 2016.

Furthermore, a lot happens in a year! If you kept a day planner, journal or even a wall calendar full of important dates, take a moment to flip through it before you get started on the following exercises.

If you've never done self-reflection like this before, you'll likely be surprised at how intense it can get. After a few questions, it will feel as though thoughts and feelings about your year have been waiting to spill out of you, and it's healthy to release them onto the page.

It's also important to note that by January 15, 95% of people have already given up on their New Year resolutions. That's a heavy majority, and you better believe that the same majority gives up on their goals year after year.

Imagine being part of the 5% that actually achieves the goals they set for themselves. In the next section, I share how this type of review shined a harsh spotlight on a few problems I was keeping in my life. Because I repeat this exercise every year, I caught myself making the exact same mistakes for three years running! And sadly, my example is the rule, not the exception.

As you perform the following reflections and review, I want you to keep a set of running questions in your mind: *What if I actually solved this problem this year? How great would that feel? What would be the resulting effects if I clear this up once and for all?*

If you want to be part of the 5% club — that small percentage of people who actually create change and success in their lives — you must be determined to not only examine what is and what isn't working in your life, but also correct it.

If you would like examples for any of the prompts in this section, please visit my blog series, *New Year for a New You*[2] to find suggestions and examples.

---

[2] HTTP://WWW.MARKETYOURCREATIVITY.COM/2015/01/A-NEW-YEAR-FOR-A-NEW-YOU-7-DAY-SERIES-FINALE/

20 | end year review | 15

WHAT ARE YOUR FAVORITE MEMORIES OF 2015?

 WHAT WAS TIME VERY WELL SPENT?

 WHAT WAS MONEY VERY WELL SPENT?

WHAT DID YOU ACCOMPLISH OR COMPLETE?

DID YOU MAKE ANY PROGRESS ON BIG LIFE GOALS?

20 | end year review | 15

WHAT FELT SUCCESSFUL ABOUT 2015?

DID YOU OVERCOME ANY OBSTACLES?

WHAT DID YOU LEARN ABOUT YOURSELF?

WHO NURTURED AND SUPPORTED YOU?

WHO DID YOU ENJOY NURTURING AND SUPPORTING?

YOUR BEST YEAR 2016 BY LISA JACOBS

20 | end year review | 15

WHAT WAS YOUR BIGGEST CHALLENGE OF 2015?

 WHAT WAS TIME WASTED THIS YEAR?

WHAT WOULD (OR WOULDN'T) YOU CHANGE ABOUT HOW YOU HANDLED IT?

 WHAT WAS MONEY WASTED THIS YEAR?

DO YOU HAVE UNFINISHED BUSINESS LEFT TO ATTEND TO?

YOUR BEST YEAR 2016 BY LISA JACOBS

20 | end year review | 15

DO YOU HAVE ANY OUTSTANDING GOALS?

DID YOU KEEP ANY BAD HABITS?

WHAT WAS YOUR WORST SETBACK?

WHAT HELD YOU BACK THIS YEAR?

HOW DID YOU HOLD YOURSELF BACK?

NEW YEAR POLICIES AND PLANNING

Every year on my blog, I lead a series titled: *A New Year for a New You: 7 Days of Review*, and this past year the week-long reflection took on a life all its own.

During the series, I offer readers a new list of prompts and review questions each day. I then blog my answers and thoughts from the previous day before issuing the next set of prompts.

When I write that series, I always go back on previous years to collect questions and collect my ideas for the new year. I was working on day two (*reviewing 2014*), when I got a wake-up call that would shape my whole year.

Most people don't have the advantage of reviewing their previous goals and challenges, but this year I was fortunate enough to have a 3-year public record of my own (this will be the fourth year the series runs).

When I reviewed my past 7-day series to collect questions for the current year's time wasted / biggest challenges / worst setbacks post, I found that my answers for 2013 review matched exactly what I planned to talk about in the 2014 review. I looked back a year further and found the same challenges / setbacks / bad habits from the 2012 review! I couldn't believe my own eyes …

I was keeping my problems year after year.

As I read back over *three years' worth* of the same relationship problems, financial setbacks and bad habits, I got emotional. That moment still makes me tear up to this day. It broke my heart that I wasn't making positive changes for myself; that I was too scared to make the tough choices for a better life.

After that day's review, I wrote the saddest, most grumbly post I've ever shared on my blog. And I think that's what made it so important. I hate to complain and dwell in the shadows, though I know it's the prequel to change.

As I said in the introduction, I've learned that we sometimes get very comfortable with our obstacles, for one reason or another:

- We like the nurturing attention it brings from the outside world;
- We're addicted to the dramatics an unsolved problem adds to our life; or
- **(Most likely) We feel overwhelmed, uncertain and too scared to take the first step in the right direction.**

This book is designed to make that first step in the right direction an easy one to take. I made the tough choices this year, and the first step in the right direction was owning my agreement to the problems I was keeping.

You are one-half of every relationship that you don't love or enjoy. You're one-half of every argument, loving exchange, passive-aggressive wiggle and direct confrontation that happens in your life. You're one-half of every good relationship, and one-half of every bad one.

It's entirely your responsibility to move things in the right direction or quit what's not working altogether.

One of the hardest decisions you'll ever face is choosing whether to walk away or try harder.

Here's to communicating your needs, boundaries and expectations in 2016! It's time to create some policies for your life and business.

Part of my coaching and writing is to teach creatives better business practices. An important business practice is to not let others manage your time or energy. *Ever*. I write and enforce my own policies each year with love, so that I may provide the best service and value for all concerned.

I strongly suggest you do the same. Use the following prompts that apply to your life and business, and feel free to leave the ones that don't. Turn your answers into canned responses that you can email to anyone who seems unclear about the boundaries concerning your time, attention, and energy.

YOUR BEST YEAR 2016 BY LISA JACOBS

20 | *new year policies* | 16

THE BEST WAY TO REACH ME:	THE BEST TIME TO REACH ME:
HOW I PREFER TO BE TREATED:	WHAT I WILL NOT TOLERATE:
ON PARTNERSHIPS, TRADES, AND COLLABORATIONS:	FOR THOSE SEEKING MY TIME OR MY WORK FOR FREE:
MY HOURS OF AVAILABILITY:	MY PRICING POLICIES:
ON REFUNDS AND RETURNS:	ON SHIPPING AND DELIVERY:
CUSTOMER SERVICE GUARANTEE:	CONFIDENTIALITY AGREEMENT:

20 | new year planning | 16

The next set of prompts are designed to help you set intentions for the New Year. I like to do this exercise before setting any major goals or resolutions to clarify what I really want to create in the coming months.

> ❝ YOU DON'T WANT TO GET TO THE TOP OF THE LADDER ONLY TO FIND OUT YOU HAD IT LEANING AGAINST THE WRONG WALL.
> – Jack Canfield

What do you want from 2016? Consider the five pillars of a harmonic life, as taught in *Harmonic Wealth: The Secret of Attracting the Life You Want* by James Arthur Ray: (1.) Financial, (2.) Spiritual, (3.) Mental, (4.) Relational, and (5.) Physical.

WHAT DO YOU WANT TO CHANGE THIS YEAR?

FINANCIAL:

SPIRITUAL:

MENTAL:

PHYSICAL:

RELATIONAL:

new year planning

Our main objective for annual planning is to break outworn patterns and bad habits. In order to get the results you want this year, you'll need to replace what's *not* working in your life with better habits that will create change.

Next, we're going to apply each change and desire you noted in the previous exercise to the following list. I've gathered these questions from *Money Master the Game: 7 Simple Steps to Financial Freedom* by Tony Robbins.

On the next page, you'll find a chart titled, "How Will You Create the Results You Want?" Refer to the previous page and your five pillar goals, and then answer the following questions for each:

- **What do I really want?** This is your vision for change, so write in the goal itself by briefly summarizing what you hope to improve in each pillar of life. For example, a financial goal might be: "Increase income by 20%."

- **Why is it important?** The answer to this uncovers the value and driving force behind your goal. For example, I want to increase my income by 20% to "reduce debt, and add fun and comfort" to my life.

- **How will I get it?** This is particularly important: these are the methods by which you will create change. For example, I will increase my income to reduce debt, and add fun and comfort to my life by "completing 2 unfinished projects while working a steady 30-hour week."

- **What is preventing it?** These are the obstacles standing in your way, or why you haven't already achieved this goal. In my example, I have "unfinished business and unreliable working hours" to correct.

- **How will I know it worked?** This is how you measure your progress. In my example, I would "earn $400 more each month."

YOUR BEST YEAR 2016 BY LISA JACOBS

20 | *new year planning* | 16

HOW WILL YOU CREATE THE RESULTS YOU WANT?

FINANCIAL:	SPIRITUAL:	MENTAL:	PHYSICAL:	RELATIONAL:
WHAT I WANT:	WHAT I WANT:	WHAT I WANT:	WHAT I WANT:	WHAT I WANT:
WHY DO I WANT IT?	WHY DO I WANT IT?	WHY DO I WANT IT?	WHY DO I WANT IT?	WHY DO I WANT IT?
HOW WILL I GET IT?	HOW WILL I GET IT?	HOW WILL I GET IT?	HOW WILL I GET IT?	HOW WILL I GET IT?
WHAT PREVENTS IT?	WHAT PREVENTS IT?	WHAT PREVENTS IT?	WHAT PREVENTS IT?	WHAT PREVENTS IT?
HOW WILL I KNOW?	HOW WILL I KNOW?	HOW WILL I KNOW?	HOW WILL I KNOW?	HOW WILL I KNOW?

📄 IF I KNEW I COULD NOT FAIL, I WOULD …

Words cannot express how powerful this exercise is, and it's time for you to think up your wildest, most amazing dreams imaginable.

Last year, I published a blog post titled, "If I Knew I Could Not Fail, I Would …" in which I listed all of the things I would do right now if I knew I could not fail. I forced myself to dream big and think outside the box. I wrote down everything I could think of, but I could only think of four items:

1. Focus all of my efforts on group coaching
2. Lead live, in-person workshops for groups of 100+
3. Host a women's retreat for 20 creatives
4. Start a podcast

To be honest with you, I posted that list for the sake of putting it out there; I wanted to demonstrate how fun the blog topic was. But in response to the article, one of my previous clients said:

"You should do all those things on your list even if you might fail at one or two."

And she was right. Of course she was right! Not only do I coach next-level business, my *own* business was built on a passion for growth and expansion. I constantly envision ways to improve and upgrade my day; it's my nature. So why hadn't I gone for these big dreams?

I guess I was just … scared? Waiting for permission? Hoping to be recognized and validated? Looking for a big break? And those things are exactly what I coach my clients not to do. I certainly could not leave my career wish list hanging. It was time for a dose of my own medicine.

I went for the one I wanted the most: I planned a women's retreat alongside an amazing line-up of inspirational leaders in our field. I reached out to my favorite creatives, pitched my idea, and they all said, "YES!" In February 2015, we met in a luxurious, oceanfront home and lead an amazing group of creatives in Charleston, South Carolina. I had the professional time of my life.

Moreover, I realized the retreat answered a deeper craving. So, I looked to answer more.

What are you truly craving?

Over the course of the year, the "If I Knew I Could Not Fail" experiment evolved into this question: What am I truly craving? And of the biggest cravings I had in online business was for a deeper connection.

I'm a creative business consultant, and when I feel a big moment coming in a session — a moment in which my natural intuition is about to align what is out-of-sync in my client's life, I have to look up into the webcam during the call (away from my client's face), so she can have eye-to-eye contact with me when I deliver that important message. Only one of us gets to truly connect during that powerful moment, and since she's the client, it's always her.

The screen gets in the way of a real connection. It's where I look at my webcam so we can pretend I'm looking into your eyes. It's where I pretend I'm dressed to the nines while I deliver my greatest blog post, when I've really just popped out of bed. It's where I share my sunlit side.

> " WE ALWAYS ENVY OTHERS, COMPARING OUR SHADOWS TO THEIR SUNLIT SIDES.
> — *Margaret George*

I craved a deeper connection, and the creative retreat — where I was able to meet people face-to-face, look into their eyes, and feel the magic in the room — was only the beginning.

Truth be told, this work-at-home business can be lonely. I've missed building, brainstorming, troubleshooting, and goofing off with my co-workers. I've missed the feelings that come from working partnerships that evolve into comfortable friendships. So in addition to the retreat, and beyond that first "If I Knew I Could Not Fail" list, I created The Luminaries Club[3] and taught to thousands on CreativeLive.[4]

---

[3] HTTP://WWW.MARKETYOURCREATIVITY.COM/LUMINARIES-CLUB/

[4] HTTPS://WWW.CREATIVELIVE.COM/INSTRUCTOR/LISA-JACOBS

If I knew I could not fail, I would ...

WHAT ARE SOME THINGS YOU COULD BE DOING THAT YOU'VE BEEN AFRAID TO TRY?

HOW CAN YOU STRETCH YOUR COMFORT ZONE?

WHAT IF YOU FAILED? WHAT'S THE WORST-CASE SCENARIO?

WHAT *HUGE* LIFE GOALS WILL YOU WORK TOWARD?

WHAT IF YOU SUCCEEDED? THE BEST-CASE SCENARIO:

IS IT WORTH IT TO TRY?

If I knew I could not fail, I would ...

> THERE IS FREEDOM WAITING FOR YOU, ON THE BREEZES OF THE SKY, AND YOU ASK, "WHAT IF I FALL?"
>
> OH BUT MY DARLING, WHAT IF YOU FLY? – Erin Hanson

What am I truly craving?

THE POWER OF 3'S

It's important to celebrate the changes in your life and the goals you are achieving. It's equally important to take responsibility for the areas that are not improving, and at least move that needle a little for the better.

Two of the biggest challenges my blog readers face are: getting more traffic and making more sales. And if you're anything like I was, you're showing up year after year in business, doing the same things and expecting different results. Let me save you the five years it took me to learn this lesson: That strategy doesn't work! Yet almost every creative I encounter is stuck in that very rut.

I started this year determined to move the needle. I was committed to making changes in my life once and for all, in both life and business.

Let me turn the tables on you the same way I love to turn them on myself:

WHAT RESULTS WERE YOU EXPECTING IN 2015?

FOR THOSE GOALS YOU DIDN'T MEET, WHY DO YOU THINK YOU DIDN'T ACHIEVE THEM?

Rather than trying to create sales (which by the way, is impossible), aim to create repetition of positive results so that you can learn from your own performance. Otherwise, you'll set yourself up for disappointment when you create a big promotion and expect the rest of the world to do their part.

Of course you're going to *hope* your marketing efforts bring results, but if they don't, it's your job to figure out why not and do better next time.

I notice that the more I repeat promotions and techniques in business, the more I learn from them. I repeat the same seasonal sales, blogging themes, marketing campaigns and *Your Best Year* planners every year, and every year what I've repeated performs better than it did in the previous year.

Repetition = an easy way to measure success.

It's funny how long we'll repeat what's *not* working in our lives, all the while truly, madly, deeply wishing for change. The time has come to create repetition (in the form of better habits and new techniques) to grow what *is* working in our lives.

As you plan for 2016, don't try to fix the slow seasons. There's no fix for them! Instead, focus on the seasons in which your business thrives and make a plan for growing *that* success.

If holiday arts shows make up your best season, schedule the majority of your marketing efforts around it: write blog posts about where you'll be, Instagram from the shows, share what's running out of stock and what people are scooping up. In other words, use what's already working to its fullest potential.

This leads me to the Power of 3's, a concept I created earlier this year. It's helped me to achieve my most productive, most profitable, and biggest breakthrough year of all time.

Typical life and business advice will tell you to make a 6-month, 1-year, 5-year and 10-year plan. That's just never worked for me. *At all*. Why? Because I don't have a traditional career with a foreseeable trajectory. I've chased big dreams because it seemed like what I was *supposed* to do next, only to find out that I hated the work! That throws most conventional 10-year plans out the window.

Instead, I decided to work in 3's, and more specifically: 3 weeks, 3 months, and 3 years.

First, I look at what I would like to accomplish with the year I'm in, and I do this every 3 months until it ends (January, April, June, September). I'm going to prompt you to do the same all year long through your work and review in this book.

Then, I ask myself: If I stayed on this course, where would it get me in 3 years? I make a projection of growth and income to ensure I like where my plan leads.

Next, I ask: What do I have to do in the next 3 months to get started on this plan? This becomes a working progress log.

Finally, what will I have to do in the next 3 weeks to make progress? From there, and as my husband always chants …

NOTHING TO IT BUT TO DO IT!

Before I lead you through your own Power of 3's exercise, I want to talk about the shadow side of progress: procrastination, hesitation, fear, and …

Self-sabotage and your creative career

Earlier this year, I was having a talk with one of my clients who was going through a difficult time, and she was reflecting on some bad habits and a bout of self-sabotage. I don't know about you, but I can absolutely relate.

In fact, I can't seem to get myself off the feast-or-famine cycle. For years, I've either been buzzing with energy or entirely burnt out. I've been prosperous or poor, overweight or too thin, on the fast track to success or on the edge of failure. The sad truth is, extremes don't bother me as much as boredom does.

My client was explaining how she leaves everything until the last minute and how it's a pattern that's gone on for most of her life.

As creatives, we ride an emotional, physical and mental roller coaster with every project we create and (self-imposed) deadline we face.

Meanwhile, new ideas are fun. When I get a new idea, I'll fill a whole section in my notebook about it, draw out large project maps, and talk about it all day to whomever will listen.

Then comes project realization, major effort is required, and overwhelming obstacles appear on your path. None of that is very fun. During the new idea stage, we feel our best and brightest. Then, things tend to get very mucky and don't feel so bright and pleasant anymore.

This is the biggest hazard to all of our careers.

While I face a lot of the same issues with self-sabotage, I wonder how much of it is me trying to harm myself versus a simple lack of self-management. I'm starting to think that calling it "self-sabotage" is actually kicking ourselves while we're down. But really, how many of us are raised to self-manage?

I notice that a lot of my clients come to me with the same questions:

- What do I focus on?
- How do I keep at it?
- How do I prioritize and self-motivate?

In planning the private retreat we held earlier this year, co-host Bonnie Christine and I were discussing who would cover what topics in our presentations, based on our attendee's needs. She had a list of things she was going to help with and answer, and I asked to cover the above issues (on what and how to focus). She said in passing, "Good – I don't know how to explain that part; I just get it done." And I'm telling you, you wouldn't believe how much Bonnie gets done!

Her saying that stuck with me so that I kept thinking about it; I'm still thinking about it. How do some people just "get it done" when I have to create all kinds of systems and explanations and rationalizations to keep myself going?

At our retreat, Bonnie mentioned in her presentation that she comes from a family of entrepreneurs. That was my a-ha! moment. While I'm sure she has the same struggles as many creatives face, on some level, she was also raised to self-manage.

What if, by saying we self-sabotage, we're actually making things worse on ourselves? What if you approach your year as if you're learning to self-manage instead?

Before this, you've likely never worked without a boss before. It's incredibly difficult to show up with good intentions of productivity, and then wing it!

If you're scooping up what you've read so far like it's a hot fudge sundae, what you need most is a manager. My husband is so good at getting things done, I often say to him, "Will you be my manager?" - Picture me as wild-eyed and desperate as the baby bird in the children's book, *Are You My Mother?* because it's a great metaphor for how I feel sometimes. He always laughs and says, "That will never work." And I end up back at square one.

However, and in lieu of an actual business manager, I present to you the next best solution!

Your current goal is your new manager.

To put theory into practice, I want you to pull one of your big dreamy goals from your "If I Knew I Could Not Fail" list. It's going to become your new business manager.

Next, I am going to show you how to reverse-engineer it, and ultimately create it, using the power of 3's.

> AMBITION, I HAVE COME TO BELIEVE, IS THE MOST PRIMAL AND SACRED FUNDAMENT OF OUR BEING. TO FEEL AMBITION AND TO ACT UPON IT IS TO EMBRACE THE UNIQUE CALLING OF OUR SOULS. NOT TO ACT UPON THAT AMBITION IS TO TURN OUR BACKS ON OURSELVES AND ON THE REASON FOR OUR EXISTENCE.
> — *Steven Pressfield*

YOUR BIG GOAL:

#1 FAST-FORWARD TO THE TIME IT'S ALREADY COMPLETED. HOW DID YOU MAKE IT HAPPEN? WHAT ACTIONS GOT YOU THERE?

#2 FILL IN THE DISTANCE BETWEEN WHERE YOU ARE NOW AND WHERE YOU WANT TO BE (I.E., ZERO, 25%, 50%, 75%, ETC.):

| STARTING FROM SCRATCH | HALF-WAY POINT | GOAL COMPLETE |

#3 WHAT'S WORKED SO FAR, GETTING YOU CLOSER TO THE GOAL?

#4 BRAINSTORM NEW THINGS YOU MIGHT TRY TO MAKE IT HAPPEN:

#5 ASSIGN A DEADLINE TO GET THIS GOAL 100% COMPLETE:

THE POWER OF 3'S

YOUR BIG GOAL:

WHAT RESULTS DO YOU ANTICIPATE FROM ACHIEVING THIS?

IF YOU STAYED ON THIS COURSE (TRIPLED THESE RESULTS AND KEPT GROWING IN THIS DIRECTION), WHERE WOULD YOU BE IN 3 YEARS?

IF YOU LIKE THOSE RESULTS:

WHAT DO YOU HAVE TO COMPLETE IN THE NEXT 3 MONTHS TO GET STARTED ON THAT?

WHAT DO YOU HAVE TO COMPLETE IN THE NEXT 3 WEEKS TO MAKE PROGRESS?

YOUR BEST YEAR 2016 BY LISA JACOBS

THE POWER OF 3'S

I'M GOING TO _____

BY _____   YOUR BIG GOAL

DUE DATE

MY DESIRED RESULTS ARE _____
_____
_____

MY CURRENT RESULTS ARE _____
_____
_____

*I am grateful for all that I have,
accepting of all that I don't,
and actively creating all that I want.*

BEST-CASE SCENARIO (IF I MEET MY GOAL) _____
_____
_____

WORST-CASE SCENARIO (IF I DON'T) _____
_____
_____

THE POWER OF 3'S

YOUR BIG GOAL:

TO-DO (NEXT 3 MONTHS):

DUE DATE:

TO-DO (NEXT 3 WEEKS):

DUE DATE:

DUE DATE:

DUE DATE:

NEXT SET OF GOALS:

⚙️ WHAT IF I HAVE A MULTI-FACETED BUSINESS?

Good for you! I hope that you do. This means that you have two or more businesses online, and each has its own ideal customer (for example, I have an online shop for handmade spiritual jewelry and an educational blog for creative entrepreneurs).

If that's the case, you need to create a separate list of goals for each side of the business, and keep the annual, monthly and weekly goals separate. DO NOT JUMBLE all of your projects into one list. Each business is a different beast, and should have its own file.

My daily planner is the only place I allow my two businesses to meet because it's where I list actionable tasks that need taken care of that day. I may focus different days, or even different hours of the same day, on the tasks I need to complete for each side of business.

QUESTION EVERYTHING ELSE YOU DO

Anytime you start fussing over your schedule or looming to-do list, I want you to question what you're doing, and more importantly, WHY you're doing it.

My big goal for 2015 was to welcome 500 members to my membership program, The Luminaries Club. I knew that 500 members would enable me to hire club counselors, create an ongoing support system, and have more time to make valuable educational tools and resources.

Therefore, I questioned everything on my to-do list as to whether or not it would help me reach that goal.

Will checking Facebook or Twitter 23 times/day help me welcome 500 new members? Absolutely not. That's why I'm rarely there anymore. Will Pinterest help me welcome 500 new members? A little bit. I give it about 20 minutes per day. Will writing an epic blog post that gets pinned 1,000 times help me to achieve my goal? *You know it.* That's the work I need to focus on!

♛ PRIORITIZE YOUR BIG IDEAS

Before I send you off to do some actual goal-setting, I want to first discuss productivity and priority in your schedule.

If you're in online business, you've likely heard of the Pareto principle (aka the 80/20 rule) which states that (from Wikipedia), "For many events, roughly 80% of the effects come from 20% of the causes." For example — and those of you who have an email list will know this to be true, 80% of your revenue comes from 20% of your customers.

The reason this rule is examined in the online world is because it's a hack for doing more of what matters to your bottom line. If 20% of your working hours produce 80% of your results, then that means that the other 80% of the time you spend produces only 20% of your desired results. How would your results improve if you focused all of your attention on the 20% of work that adds to 80% of your bottom line? That's what we're going to explore in this section.

Ask yourself the following questions to find out which 20% of your applied efforts are producing 80% of your desired results:

WHAT WAS YOUR BEST CREATIVE PAYDAY OF ALL TIME?

WHERE ARE YOU INVESTING TIME & ENERGY WITHOUT GENERATING A RETURN?

Therein lies the answer to figuring out which of your efforts are producing the results you want. For example, to my best creative payday, I answered the private group coaching concentrates I offer. In just three months, it produced 80% of my income for a focused 20% of my time.

To what's costing me, I answered my tendency to hesitate on big decisions, and the rule rang true again. Him-hawing on major decisions that will take my career to the next level was certainly eating up the other 80% of my time and producing 20% of my results.

Focus is a muscle that can be strengthened.

Let's be brutally honest with each other for a moment. How much of your time is spent checking email? How many times do you visit Pinterest a day? How often do you check stats? How many times have you visited Facebook this morning alone?

The time-wasting temptations for an online business owner are many! Experiment by turning your computer off for one full day, and count how many times you try to take a detour just to "check" or "look something up." It boggles the mind how our newly developed, yet incessant need-to-know eats up our day.

Now imagine what would happen if you could eliminate all of these time-wasters during your working hours. Imagine how far you would get in one calendar year if you only focused on the 20% of your work that produces 80% of your desired results.

I ask you to entertain the idea that each of us has a reserve bank of willpower, and that once it's been depleted, it's spent until it has the time to replenish itself.

For example, have you ever had a highly productive Monday? The kind of day that makes you think, "Look at all I've done! I'm going to knock it out of the ballpark this week!" Only to wake up on Tuesday and find yourself mentally and physically spent; so much so that it's virtually impossible to get anything done? That's because we have a reserve of willpower, and when it's spent, you're out of fuel. An empty willpower reserve is the black hole of productive energy.

To build a business that serves you, to be an incredibly efficient operation, you need to learn how to spend your time wisely (homing in on that 20%), refill your reserves more quickly, and expand that bank so that it can hold more of your sacred energy.

How to train your focus muscle

Think of building your focus like training for long distance running. In order to improve, to go farther at a faster pace, you would gradually (and regularly) push yourself just past your personal breaking point. If I can comfortably run 2 miles in 20 minutes today, tomorrow I will have to run 2.1 miles in the same time to begin to build up my strength and endurance.

The same goes for your personal reserves of willpower. That focus muscle needs to be trained for increased strength and endurance, and the best way to do this is to work in timed sessions.

In fact as I write this, I have a kitchen timer counting down my 50-minute interval of pure focus. Having a timer counting down my work hours helps me stay on track.

Working from home (and on the computer, no less) is full of distractions! The rule is that while the timer is on, I can only work on the project at hand: no snacks, no bathroom breaks, no internet clicking, no phone calls, etc. When my time is up, I take a short break, and then I set it again.

When I first set out to increase my focus, I allotted at least two hours for laser-focused production time. Now I'm up to at least five timed hours per weekday. In the beginning, the level of energy or resistance you have for a task should determine how long the timer will be set between breaks. Here is a guide:

- Difficult tasks and grudge work: 15 minutes
- Work you're resisting, but perfectly capable of doing: 25 minutes
- Work you enjoy: 50 minutes

The results from a laser-focused, timed work sessions are truly amazing! Try it for just one week to see how much you can accomplish.

SECTION 2
PREPARE

YOUR BEST YEAR 2016

by Lisa Jacobs

MAKE IT HAPPEN ALREADY

Are you tired of wishing and hoping, and ready to make it happen *already*?

The single biggest threat to our goals is setting vague, distant deadlines for their completion. When I wrote my first "If I Knew I Could Not Fail, I Would …" list, I didn't plan to do any of the items on the list anytime soon!

When I read the comment from a reader (and former client) who told me I should do all of those things even if I might fail at one or two, it knocked me out of my chair. I couldn't believe how right she was.

> "GREAT PEOPLE DO THINGS BEFORE THEY'RE READY. THEY DO THINGS BEFORE THEY KNOW THEY CAN DO IT. DOING WHAT YOU'RE AFRAID OF, GETTING OUT OF YOUR COMFORT ZONE, TAKING RISKS LIKE THAT — THAT IS WHAT LIFE IS.
>
> YOU MIGHT FIND OUT SOMETHING ABOUT YOURSELF THAT'S REALLY SPECIAL. IF YOU'RE NOT GOOD, WHO CARES? YOU TRIED SOMETHING. NOW YOU KNOW SOMETHING ABOUT YOURSELF.
>
> — Amy Poehler

I didn't feel ready yet, but I accepted the challenge. I got right to work on, not one of my big goals, but all four of them! I launched a group coaching program and worked with a handful amazing clients. I hosted a women's retreat titled, Movers & Makers. I taught a CreativeLive class to thousands of people live. After looking into it further, I didn't want a podcast at the time, but I hosted live end-month chats in its place.

It was the most successful year of my creative career yet! And it all happened because I started before I thought I was ready. I never would've gone for those things last year if I hadn't shared my list and listened to the feedback it received, but I'm so glad I did! I now consider the "If I Knew I Could Not Fail" list a necessary exercise to be completed every year.

THE SECRET TO SUCCESS

In 2015, I celebrated my fifth year in business, and I couldn't be more excited about the creative career that I built from the ground up! I've made thousands of sales at the Energy Shop on Etsy, I've quadrupled my blog traffic, my Marketing email list boasts tens of thousands of subscribers, and I've reached my start-up goal of being a full-time work-at-home Mom. *But, I've been keeping a secret.*

For all the marketing strategy, shop fundamentals and selling tips I share, there's one secret ingredient that I often leave out of the recipe. Though I KNOW it's the guiding force behind my success, I've always considered it a given — the thing everyone already knows is required.

However, I now realize that just because everyone knows there's a necessary ingredient doesn't mean they always remember to include it. It still needs to be listed on the recipe! And that's what this section serves to do for your best year.

We often look at the online empires of others and marvel at the success they've found: hundreds of thousands of followers, thousands of sales and a steady flurry of sharing and support. It's very easy to get caught in the comparison game right then and there and tell yourself: *I don't have anywhere near that reach! I'll never make it in this business.*

In other words, we tell ourselves that the successful people around us have something we don't, as if the deck's been stacked in their favor. When you stumble upon a seemingly overnight success in the form of a best-selling shop or popular blogger, it's easy to be blinded by their fame.

I've cracked the code on this. If another business seemingly finds instant success, it's possible this is their fifth try in business (as the Energy Shop was mine). It's possible that they bought an email list or an already-established brand. It's possible that a few Etsy top-sellers are buying their own sales (where you see pages and pages of "anonymous" reviews, covered by one or two buyers' feedback on top). The bloggers that appear to be big stars overnight most likely bought an already-existing domain or redirected traffic from another well-established blog they'd been working on for years.

Don't compare yourself to them! The rest of us start with our very first customer or our very first reader. And from there, we just. kept. building. The REAL secret to my own success is this:

Persistence

I am constantly forcing myself to keep going when it seems like nobody's …

- buying,
- listening,
- reading,
- caring,
- supporting or
- sharing

And it happens *all the time*. Sometimes, even when my business is thriving on paper, to me it still feels like nobody's out there.

Therefore, I've created some tips and exercises to help you stick with your big goals all year through. A lot of what we talk about here will be transferred into your annual system (next section), so let's get to work.

#1 CREATE AND REMIND

Brace yourself: Sometimes you'll release your glorious, passionate creation into the world and nobody even notices it's there! When this happens, the majority of creatives will ditch the new creation out of sheer disappointment.

Don't be one of them! It's not only your job to create the product, it's also your job to help it find success. For every new project you release, launch it with a 3-6 month marketing plan. As any good marketer will tell you, the release date is actually the *middle* of a campaign.

People need time to consider the offer, but don't let them forget about it!

YOUR PROJECT/NEW PRODUCT:
COMPLETION DEADLINE:

#1 WHAT DATE WILL YOU LAUNCH/RELEASE THIS PRODUCT?
BEST RESULTS = 6 WEEKS IN ADVANCE, NO FEWER THAN 2 WEEKS

#2 6 WEEKS IN ADVANCE: ANNOUNCE PRODUCT & RELEASE DATE. WHAT DATE WILL YOU MAKE THE ANNOUNCEMENT AND WHERE?
BEST RESULTS = A DAY-LONG EVENT ACROSS BLOG, SOCIAL MEDIA CHANNELS, CREATIVE NETWORK

#3 2 WEEKS IN ADVANCE: AT LEAST 4 PROMOTIONAL BLOG POSTS AND 8 SOCIAL MEDIA ANNOUNCEMENTS COUNTING DOWN
BEST RESULTS = INFORMATIONAL & FUN: SNEAK PEEKS, BEHIND-THE-SCENES, LAUNCH PREP, ETC.

#4 LAUNCH! HOW WILL YOU CELEBRATE IT & WHERE?
BEST RESULTS = ALL DAY LONG & EVERYWHERE!

#5 REMIND: SCHEDULE FOLLOW-UP POSTS AND ANNOUNCEMENTS, SPECIAL PROMOTIONS, AND LAST-CHANCE DEALS
BEST RESULTS = CONTINUE TO PROMOTE AT LEAST 3-MONTHS POST-LAUNCH, NO LESS THAN 6 WEEKS

Secret to success (cont'd)

#2 DISSOLVE ATTACHMENTS TO THE DESIRED OUTCOME

As you can see from the previous exercise, it sometimes takes 3-to 6-months to know if your newly released product or project is a success or a failure. Therefore, it's important to dissolve your attachments (and anxiety) to the desired outcome of a project launch.

My favorite example of this were the monthly Create Happy Hours I started hosting in August 2014. The first live webinar boasted nearly 100 sign-ups, which is phenomenal for a self-hosted, self-promoted call. I expected a huge turnout and even hired someone to help moderate the hour-long session.

When only a dozen people attended live, I was ready to quit the idea altogether. It was easy to write it off as something people just weren't that interested in and deem it a waste of time.

Instead, I decided to commit to six months of live calls, announcing the topics and air time so that people could save the date. The live attendance never did improve much, but I did find a way to repurpose the calls. Each month, I turned that topic into a course and challenge for members of The Luminaries Club.

It worked out brilliantly because I was able to share insider secrets live for those who could attend while laying the groundwork for challenges I was going to create anyway inside the membership program. The project was able to find success in a different way after I'd dissolved my attachment to the original desired outcome.

#3 TRACK YOUR PROGRESS

One of the most empowering things I've ever done in business was share my income reports for a year of full disclosure. It helped me remember *why* I started a business and the original goal I'd set back in 2010 when I began this journey.

Creative businesses can feel like a lot of giving without any return. That's why, in 2016, we'll be tracking progress all year long.

Secret to success (cont'd)

#4 MEET YOUR DEADLINES, NO MATTER WHAT

Publicly announce your deadlines weeks before the project's release so that everyone will know when to expect it. And then, meet that deadline no matter what.

The hardest project I have ever launched was The Luminaries Club. I desperately wanted to push the deadline back, but I had been talking about its arrival for months, and I was determined to make it happen even though there were several technical issues (the day before deadline, the check-out button still wasn't working). The launch date was October 1, 2014, and I solved the last issue and wrapped production the night before at 11:56 PM. I lost my marbles in the process, but I got it done.

#5 IT'S MEANT TO BE HARD; MIGHT AS WELL GO FOR BROKE

When we meet a point of resistance, it's often in our nature to say: *I can't do this; it's too much for me.* We all know that challenge creates change. However, the majority of us are eager to surrender back to the safety of our comfort zones when the going gets tough.

Don't be one of them! Remember: it's meant to be hard. If you want to create extraordinary results, you have to first accept and complete the difficult challenges.

I refer to the month that I built The Luminaries Club as "weepy September." I was prone to sobbing in public. My patience and willpower were completely depleted. My children nicknamed me "Grumplestiltskin." I wanted nothing more than to call the whole thing quits. But then I remembered, it's meant to be hard.

If you're not willing to go broke for it, then it's not good enough yet. My most successful launches have been that passionate: I believed in the product so much that I was willing to invest, promote, sacrifice, invent … to do whatever I needed to do to make it the best that it could be and get it out into the world. You've got to deeply believe in it if you want others to do the same.

THE SUCCESS PLAN

NAME THE TOP 5 THINGS YOU WOULD LIKE TO SPEND YOUR PROFITS ON THIS YEAR...

1.
2.

ABOUT HOW MUCH
WILL EACH $ COST?

3.
4.
5.

BASED ON THAT LIST ABOVE, WHAT AMOUNT OF MONEY COULD YOU EARN IN 2016 THAT WOULD LEAVE YOU FEELING ABUNDANT, FREE, WEALTHY, CONFIDENT AND SECURE? WRITE THAT NUMBER BELOW:

BEFORE TAXES & EXPENSES:	TAKE-HOME PAY:

NEXT, LIST AT LEAST 10 THINGS YOU'RE GOING TO DO OR CREATE IN THE NEW YEAR TO MAKE THAT NUMBER A REALITY:

1.
2.
3.
4.
5.

6.
7.
8.
9.
10.

ABOUT HOW MUCH
WILL EACH $ EARN?

WHEN WILL YOU
LAUNCH/DO EACH?

THE SUCCESS PLAN

CREATIVE BUSINESS OWNERS WEAR MANY HATS. WHAT PRACTICES DO YOU HAVE IN PLACE TO BE THE BEST ...

SECRETARY:
EMPTY INBOX, CLEAR DESK, SCHEDULE & APPTS.

CREATOR:
PRODUCT AND PROJECT PRODUCTION

PROJECT MANAGER:
DEADLINES AND ORGANIZATION

AND CEO:
VISION KEEPER, GROWTH STRATEGIST

... FOR YOUR BUSINESS?
HOW OFTEN WILL YOU WEAR EACH HAT AND FOR HOW LONG?

HOW MANY DAYS WILL YOU WORK EACH WEEK?

WHAT DO YOU DO WHEN YOU'RE NOT DOING WHAT YOU'RE SUPPOSED TO BE DOING?

HOW MANY FOCUSED HOURS WILL YOU COMMIT/WORK DAY?

HOW WILL YOU CATCH & ELIMINATE TIME-WASTERS?

HOW WILL YOU ACCRUE VACATION TIME?

WHAT DO YOU NEED TO STOP DOING ONCE & FOR ALL?

ARE THERE ANY PERKS OR SPECIAL BENEFITS TO YOUR JOB?

IN 2016, I VOW TO . . .

BE LESS _____
_____
_____

BE MORE _____
_____
_____

LEARN HOW TO _____
_____
_____

BECOME MORE CONFIDENT AT _____
_____
_____

HAVE LESS _____
_____
_____

HAVE MORE _____
_____
_____

NEW HABITS FOR A NEW YOU

Simply *having* goals won't make them come true; that's what habits are for. Your goal may be to meet a certain income level this year, the habit you create is what you'll do every day to achieve it.

If you ignore a goal, but adopt the habits it requires, you'll still meet the goal. If you have a goal, but don't adopt the habits required, you'll make very little progress and fail the goal.

In other words, if my personal fitness goal was to lose ten pounds, and the habits I needed to adopt to achieve that goal were to eat clean and hit 10,000 steps everyday — even if I stopped focusing on the goal and only adopted the habits, could I expect results? Of course!

Good habits are what actually create the results. Let's look at some common goals in creative business …

- Make more money
- Get more sales
- Make more listings/products
- Get more email subscribers
- Get more website traffic/views
- Upgrade the business (better design, branding, photography, etc.)
- Work ahead

All of these goals in themselves are vague, blanket statements. To even be good goals, we'd need to make them SMART goals:

Specific ("Increase my profits by 20% this year" vs. "Make more money")
Measurable ("Find 100 new customers" vs. "Get more sales")
Action-oriented (What do you need to do? vs. what you need from customers)
Realistic (I prefer to set goals that are challenging, yet doable — a stretch)
Time-based (Give yourself a deadline)

But even SMART goals won't do the work for you. The habits you create, along with each focused hour you spend performing tasks that will help you meet your goals, is what will get you across the finish line.

Let's look at some general habits you might want to create this year in order to achieve your goals. Even if you only invested one hour per day on the following habits, you'd be getting somewhere.

- Better morning routine
- More sleep
- More progress + review check-ins
- Less distractions
- Less busywork
- Better marketing
- More exercise
- More engaging social media content
- More email subscribers
- Better copywriting

Create a new habit

Focus on one at a time. Take for example, the massive failure we watch every year as people adopt the New Year's extreme-diet-join-the-gym-cut-sugar-no-carbs-restrict-everything goal. If you overwhelm yourself with too many changes, you'll fall right back into bad patterns.

Create a routine. I love to have the habit I need to create laid out as a to-do list. When I was doing a clean-eating cleanse, the most helpful tool I had was a list of everything I needed to eat that day (and when) in order to stay on track. Anytime you can spell out the changes for yourself, do so.

Hands down, the best way to start a productive day full of better habits is to create a morning routine and stick to it! I've found that one morning hour can make or break my workday, and it starts at 7 AM. By that time, I've had two cups of coffee, and I need to see my children off to school.

With that hour, I can either do all of this:

- Review the day with my children and send them off with love and attention,
- Have a healthy breakfast and drink my first glass of water,
- Clean up the breakfast dishes and start the dishwasher,
- Start a load of laundry,
- Review my planner and the day's tasks,
- Get cleaned up and dressed,
- Make my bed, and
- Be at my desk for work by 8 AM.

Or, I do this:

Sit on the couch with my laptop checking stats and repeatedly clicking on social media sites and email.

I have to decide how I'm going to spend that hour (and 12 more like it) everyday, and I thank myself every time I make the better choice.

Track your habits. I've incorporated habit trackers into your system. Like all of our other progress reviews, it's important to know where you're succeeding and what needs more work.

Take it one day at a time. Don't let a lazy, overindulgent weekend spoil all of your efforts. If you slip off course, it only takes one good decision to get you right back on track. With bigger goals (that take longer to achieve), it's better to work every day toward long-term transformation rather than try to adhere to rigid deadlines with a "succeed or fail" mindset.

Your daily routine will help you stay (and get back) on track. Without it, you're more likely to return to outworn patterns and old habits. Set a work schedule, a workout schedule, and a chore schedule. And then challenge yourself to follow it for just one day. Then another. Then a week!

A day planner proves to be a very useful tool so that you can write down what you'd like to accomplish in advance, and cross it off when it's complete.

SCHEDULE REGULAR PROGRESS REVIEWS

The best way to ensure your progress and success this year is to make a commitment — right now — to regular reviews.

I encourage my clients to *obsess* over their goals. If you are not actively creating and enforcing new patterns, you are unconsciously falling into old ones. You're going to do either or.

In the next section, you'll gain a better understanding of this system. For now, use this suggested outline to schedule regular progress reviews into your day planner or calendar.

TO START:

- Block off vacation time and important dates for 2016 in advance
- Review your "If I Knew I Could Not Fail List"
- Name some goals for the year (next section)
- Fill out the 12-month planner based on those goals (next section)
- Create your first 3-month progress log (next section)

QUARTERLY:

- Fill out the 12-month planner (schedule now to do every 3 months)
- Create a new 3-month progress log (schedule now to do every 3 months)
- Schedule your mid-year review (June)

MONTHLY:

- Fill out your monthly goal sheet (schedule now for the 1st of each month)
- Fill out your monthly review (schedule now for the 1st of each month)

WEEKLY:

- Use your habit tracker to ensure progress
- Prioritize tasks to be completed
- Customize your schedule
- Commit to a set amount of focus hours and progress

SECTION 3
DO

YOUR BEST YEAR 2016

by Lisa Jacobs

YOUR ITINERARY FOR 2016

You can shape 2016 however you like it. The year's as moldable as a fresh block of clay. To make the most of the unlimited potential that awaits you, I like to create what I call a "project map."

A project map is a systematic brain dump created to help you make progress on your big goals. To make one, you'll need a project map book (aka a large children's drawing pad). I love these giant, 16x20" pads for project maps because they're large and require you to spread out in a clean and open space — which also attracts new inspiration and a fresh perspective.

If you're anything like me, you're likely to have several budding projects at any given time. That's good — each idea gets its own page. Title the project and write that in the center of a clean sheet of drawing paper. Everything that goes on this page must be relevant to the project at hand. Resist the temptation to jot down side notes or go off-topic.

HOW TO CREATE A PROJECT MAP

#1 WRITE THE MISSION AND/OR STARTING POINT FOR THIS PROJECT

#2 THE SCHEDULE: WHAT NEEDS DONE BY WHEN TO MEET THE DEADLINE

#3 THE INDIVIDUAL OBSTACLES YOU FACE OR "MUD" YOU'RE STUCK IN

project name
+ DEADLINE

#4 THE DETAILS + OUTLINE OF THE PROJECT ITSELF

#5 THE EXTRA POSSIBILITIES + MARKETING STRATEGIES + FUTURE POTENTIAL OF THE WORK AT HAND

START A FRESH PAGE FOR EACH PROJECT

I mention "mud" in that graphic, and I'd like to explain this further. Anytime you start a project that you've never done before, you'll encounter a lot of obstacles that will threaten to seriously slow your progress. In other words, you'll run into a whole lot of mud that is sure to make you struggle.

The most dangerous thing about the mud is that it can feel overwhelming and impossible at first. You can't avoid these muddy situations, so the only way to get past the mud is to start trudging through it. After I have a project drawn out on my map, I list the things I'll need to do, learn or tackle on the map, and then prioritize them.

Before I prompt you to create your big goals for 2016, I want to give you one final list to consider.

THIS YEAR I WANT TO …

FINISH _____

THAT THING THAT NAGS AT YOU WHEN YOU THINK OF "UNFINISHED BUSINESS"

ADD _____

HELPFUL PEOPLE, MENTORS, POSITIVE FRIENDS, TIME OFF, MORE LUXURY, FINANCIAL SECURITY

LEARN _____

A NEW BUSINESS SKILL, MARKETING STRATEGY, TECHNIQUE FOR MY CRAFT

IMPROVE _____

MY HEALTH, MY WEALTH, RELATIONSHIPS WITH THE PEOPLE I LOVE

ENHANCE _____

THOSE THINGS THAT WORKED LAST YEAR, MY SAVINGS ACCOUNT, MY PERSONAL WELLBEING

2016 TABLE OF CONTENTS

ANNUAL OBJECTIVES	57
PROGRESS LOG (QUARTER 1)	59
JANUARY	60
FEBRUARY	66
MARCH	72
PROGRESS LOG (QUARTER 2)	79
APRIL	80
MAY	86
JUNE	92
MID-YEAR REVIEW	98
PROGRESS LOG (QUARTER 3)	105
JULY	106
AUGUST	112
SEPTEMBER	118
PROGRESS LOG (QUARTER 4)	125
OCTOBER	126
NOVEMBER	132
DECEMBER	138

YOUR BEST YEAR 2016 BY LISA JACOBS

ANNUAL OBJECTIVES

FILL IN THE GOALS THAT WILL MAKE 2016 FEEL LIKE AN ABSOLUTE SUCCESS

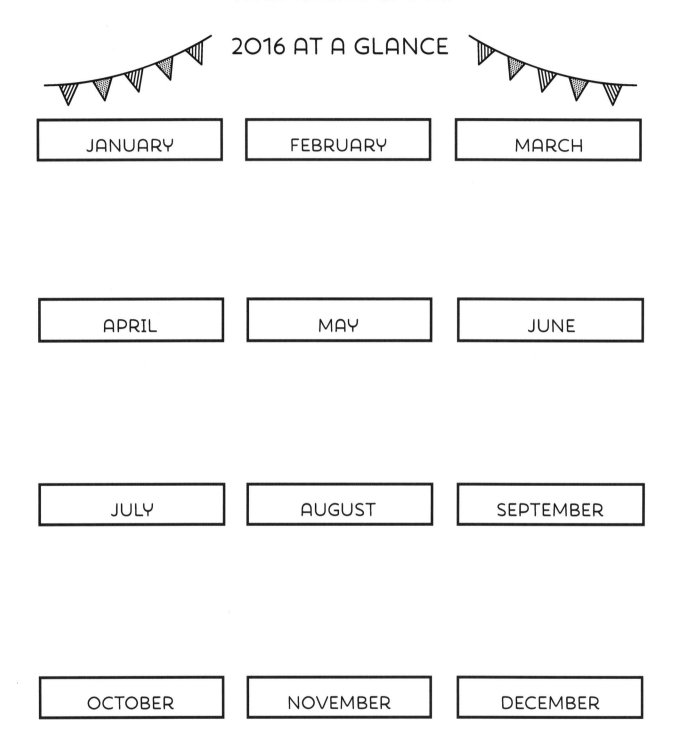

2016 AT A GLANCE

YOUR BEST YEAR 2016 BY LISA JACOBS

JANUARY • FEBRUARY • MARCH
APRIL • MAY • JUNE
JULY • AUGUST • SEPTEMBER
OCTOBER • NOVEMBER • DECEMBER

YOU HAVE A WHOLE YEAR TO MAKE IT HAPPEN! WHAT WILL YOU ACCOMPLISH WITH EACH PASSING MONTH?

YOUR BEST YEAR 2016 BY LISA JACOBS

 # PROGRESS LOG

WHAT GOALS DO YOU NEED TO COMPLETE IN THE NEXT 3 MONTHS TO STAY ON TRACK WITH YOUR ANNUAL OBJECTIVES?

 ESTIMATE THE TIME EACH PROJECT WILL TAKE & THE AMOUNT OF INCOME YOU CAN EXPECT TO EARN

DUE DATE:

FILL IN THE DISTANCE BETWEEN WHERE YOU ARE NOW AND WHERE YOU WANT TO BE (I.E., ZERO, 25%, 50%, 75%, ETC.):

JANUARY 2016

TO-DO	SUNDAY	MONDAY	TUESDAY
☐ ☐ ☐	DECEMBER 27	28	29
☐ ☐ ☐	3	4	5
☐ ☐ ☐	10	11	12
☐ ☐ ☐	17	18	19
UP NEXT	24 / 31	25	26

YOUR BEST YEAR 2016 BY LISA JACOBS

WEDNESDAY	THURSDAY	FRIDAY	SATURDAY
30	31	1	2
6	7	8	9
13	14	15	16
20	21	22	23
27	28	29	30

JANUARY 2016

MONTHLY TO-DO LIST:

☐
☐
☐

☐
☐
☐

☐
☐
☐

☐
☐
☐

PRIORITIES AND PROJECTS:

GOALS TO WORK ON:

FINANCIAL:

SPIRITUAL:

MENTAL:

RELATIONAL:

PHYSICAL:

SPECIAL EVENTS AND APPOINTMENTS TO REMEMBER THIS MONTH:

PROGRESS TRACKER (RECORD PREVIOUS MONTH'S NUMBERS):

FB   PINTEREST   EMAIL   VIEWS   SALES   [   ]   [   ]   [   ]   [   ]

___   ___   ___   ___   ___   ___   ___   ___   ___

JANUARY 2016

NEW HABIT TO ADOPT THIS MONTH:	WHAT IS IT TIME TO STOP DOING?

DECEMBER 27—JANUARY 2

PRIMARY TASKS TO COMPLETE:

NEW HABIT TRACKER:
☐ ☐ ☐ ☐ ☐ ☐ ☐

JANUARY 3—JANUARY 9

PRIMARY TASKS TO COMPLETE:

NEW HABIT TRACKER:
☐ ☐ ☐ ☐ ☐ ☐ ☐

JANUARY 10—JANUARY 16

PRIMARY TASKS TO COMPLETE:

NEW HABIT TRACKER:
☐ ☐ ☐ ☐ ☐ ☐ ☐

JANUARY 17—JANUARY 23

PRIMARY TASKS TO COMPLETE:

NEW HABIT TRACKER:
☐ ☐ ☐ ☐ ☐ ☐ ☐

JANUARY 24—JANUARY 30

PRIMARY TASKS TO COMPLETE:

NEW HABIT TRACKER:
☐ ☐ ☐ ☐ ☐ ☐ ☐

JANUARY 2016 — IN REVIEW

MEMORABLE MOMENTS:

PROJECTS COMPLETED THIS MONTH:

PROJECTS STILL IN THE WORKS:

GOAL PROGRESS:

- FINANCIAL:
- SPIRITUAL:
- MENTAL:
- RELATIONAL:
- PHYSICAL:

MOST IMPORTANT TO ME RIGHT NOW:

WHAT DO I NEED TO IMPROVE?

JANUARY 2016 — IN REVIEW

NEW HABIT I WANTED TO ADOPT:

WAS IT A SUCCESS?

IF YES:

NEXT GOOD HABIT TO ADOPT:

IF NO:

WHAT I'LL DO NEXT TO MAKE IT WORK:

WHAT WORKED WELL THIS MONTH:

I.E. POPULAR BLOG POSTS, ENGAGING SOCIAL UPDATES, WAVE OF NEW SUBSCRIBERS

AND WHY?

HOW CAN I REPEAT OR DOUBLE THESE RESULTS?

DID THIS MONTH GET ME CLOSER TO MY ANNUAL OBJECTIVES?

IF YES, HOW WILL I KEEP THAT MOMENTUM?

IF NO, WHAT WILL I DO TO GET BACK ON TRACK?

WHAT OBSTACLE(S) AM I FACING?

WHY IS IT DIFFICULT?

WHAT HAVE I TRIED (SO FAR) TO OVERCOME THE ISSUE(S)?

WHAT CAN I TRY NEXT?

FEBRUARY 2016

TO-DO	SUNDAY	MONDAY	TUESDAY
☐ ☐ ☐	JANUARY 31	1	2
☐ ☐ ☐	7	8	9
☐ ☐ ☐	14	15	16
☐ ☐ ☐	21	22	23
UP NEXT	28	29	MARCH 1

WEDNESDAY	THURSDAY	FRIDAY	SATURDAY
3	4	5	6
10	11	12	13
17	18	19	20
24	25	26	27
2	3	4	5

FEBRUARY 2016

MONTHLY TO-DO LIST:

- [ ]
- [ ]
- [ ]

- [ ]
- [ ]
- [ ]

- [ ]
- [ ]
- [ ]

- [ ]
- [ ]
- [ ]

PRIORITIES AND PROJECTS:

GOALS TO WORK ON:

FINANCIAL:

SPIRITUAL:

MENTAL:

RELATIONAL:

PHYSICAL:

SPECIAL EVENTS AND APPOINTMENTS TO REMEMBER THIS MONTH:

PROGRESS TRACKER (RECORD PREVIOUS MONTH'S NUMBERS):

FB   PINTEREST   EMAIL   VIEWS   SALES   [   ] [   ] [   ] [   ]

FEBRUARY 2016

NEW HABIT TO ADOPT THIS MONTH:	WHAT IS IT TIME TO STOP DOING?

JANUARY 31—FEBRUARY 6
PRIMARY TASKS TO COMPLETE:

NEW HABIT TRACKER:
☐ ☐ ☐ ☐ ☐ ☐ ☐

FEBRUARY 7—FEBRUARY 13
PRIMARY TASKS TO COMPLETE:

NEW HABIT TRACKER:
☐ ☐ ☐ ☐ ☐ ☐ ☐

FEBRUARY 14—FEBRUARY 20
PRIMARY TASKS TO COMPLETE:

NEW HABIT TRACKER:
☐ ☐ ☐ ☐ ☐ ☐ ☐

FEBRUARY 21—FEBRUARY 27
PRIMARY TASKS TO COMPLETE:

NEW HABIT TRACKER:
☐ ☐ ☐ ☐ ☐ ☐ ☐

FEBRUARY 28—MARCH 5
PRIMARY TASKS TO COMPLETE:

NEW HABIT TRACKER:
☐ ☐ ☐ ☐ ☐ ☐ ☐

FEBRUARY 2016 — IN REVIEW

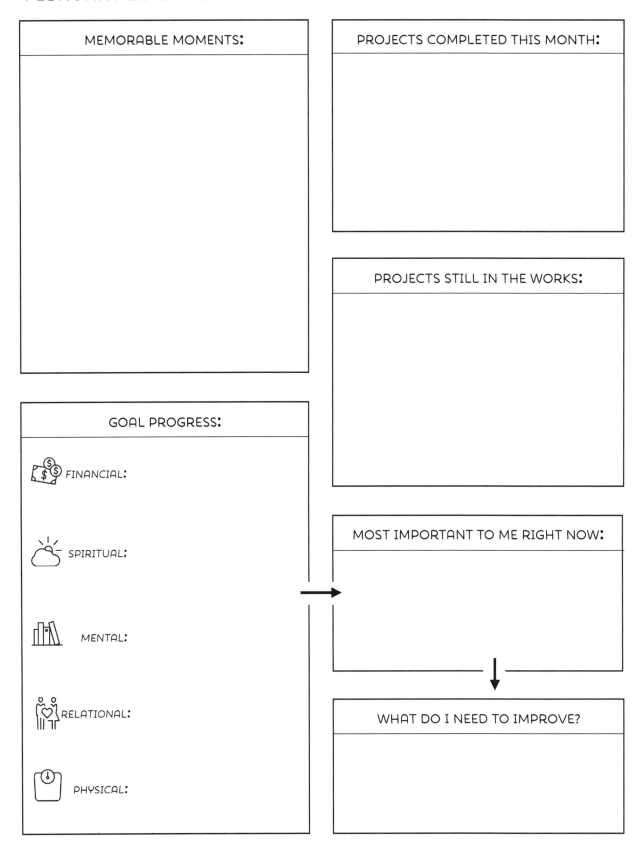

FEBRUARY 2016 — IN REVIEW

NEW HABIT I WANTED TO ADOPT:

WAS IT A SUCCESS?

IF YES:	IF NO:
NEXT GOOD HABIT TO ADOPT:	WHAT I'LL DO NEXT TO MAKE IT WORK:

DID THIS MONTH GET ME CLOSER TO MY ANNUAL OBJECTIVES?

IF YES, HOW WILL I KEEP THAT MOMENTUM?

IF NO, WHAT WILL I DO TO GET BACK ON TRACK?

WHAT WORKED WELL THIS MONTH:

I.E. POPULAR BLOG POSTS, ENGAGING SOCIAL UPDATES, WAVE OF NEW SUBSCRIBERS

AND WHY?

HOW CAN I REPEAT OR DOUBLE THESE RESULTS?

WHAT OBSTACLE(S) AM I FACING?

WHY IS IT DIFFICULT?

WHAT HAVE I TRIED (SO FAR) TO OVERCOME THE ISSUE(S)?

WHAT CAN I TRY NEXT?

MARCH 2016

TO-DO	SUNDAY	MONDAY	TUESDAY
☐ ☐ ☐	FEBRUARY 28	29	1
☐ ☐ ☐	6	7	8
☐ ☐ ☐	13	14	15
☐ ☐ ☐	20	21	22
UP NEXT	27	28	29

YOUR BEST YEAR 2016 BY LISA JACOBS

WEDNESDAY	THURSDAY	FRIDAY	SATURDAY
2	3	4	5
9	10	11	12
16	17	18	19
23	24	25	26
30	31	APRIL 1	2

MARCH 2016

MONTHLY TO-DO LIST:

☐
☐
☐

☐
☐
☐

☐
☐
☐

☐
☐
☐

PRIORITIES AND PROJECTS:

GOALS TO WORK ON:

FINANCIAL:

SPIRITUAL:

MENTAL:

RELATIONAL:

PHYSICAL:

SPECIAL EVENTS AND APPOINTMENTS TO REMEMBER THIS MONTH:

PROGRESS TRACKER (RECORD PREVIOUS MONTH'S NUMBERS):

FB   PINTEREST   EMAIL   VIEWS   SALES   [   ]   [   ]   [   ]   [   ]

MARCH 2016

| NEW HABIT TO ADOPT THIS MONTH: | WHAT IS IT TIME TO STOP DOING? |

MARCH 6 — MARCH 12

PRIMARY TASKS TO COMPLETE:

NEW HABIT TRACKER:
☐ ☐ ☐ ☐ ☐ ☐ ☐

MARCH 13 — MARCH 19

PRIMARY TASKS TO COMPLETE:

NEW HABIT TRACKER:
☐ ☐ ☐ ☐ ☐ ☐ ☐

MARCH 20 — MARCH 26

PRIMARY TASKS TO COMPLETE:

NEW HABIT TRACKER:
☐ ☐ ☐ ☐ ☐ ☐ ☐

MARCH 27 — APRIL 2

PRIMARY TASKS TO COMPLETE:

NEW HABIT TRACKER:
☐ ☐ ☐ ☐ ☐ ☐ ☐

NOTES:

MARCH 2016 — IN REVIEW

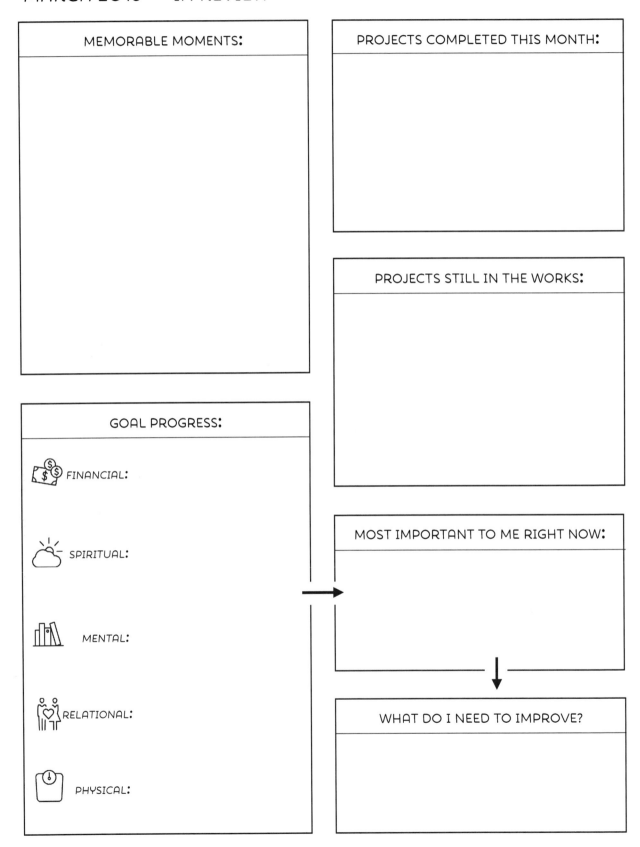

MARCH 2016 — IN REVIEW

NEW HABIT I WANTED TO ADOPT:

WAS IT A SUCCESS?

IF YES:	IF NO:
NEXT GOOD HABIT TO ADOPT:	WHAT I'LL DO NEXT TO MAKE IT WORK:

DID THIS MONTH GET ME CLOSER TO MY ANNUAL OBJECTIVES?

IF YES, HOW WILL I KEEP THAT MOMENTUM?

IF NO, WHAT WILL I DO TO GET BACK ON TRACK?

WHAT WORKED WELL THIS MONTH:

I.E. POPULAR BLOG POSTS, ENGAGING SOCIAL UPDATES, WAVE OF NEW SUBSCRIBERS

AND WHY?

HOW CAN I REPEAT OR DOUBLE THESE RESULTS?

WHAT OBSTACLE(S) AM I FACING?

WHY IS IT DIFFICULT?

WHAT HAVE I TRIED (SO FAR) TO OVERCOME THE ISSUE(S)?

WHAT CAN I TRY NEXT?

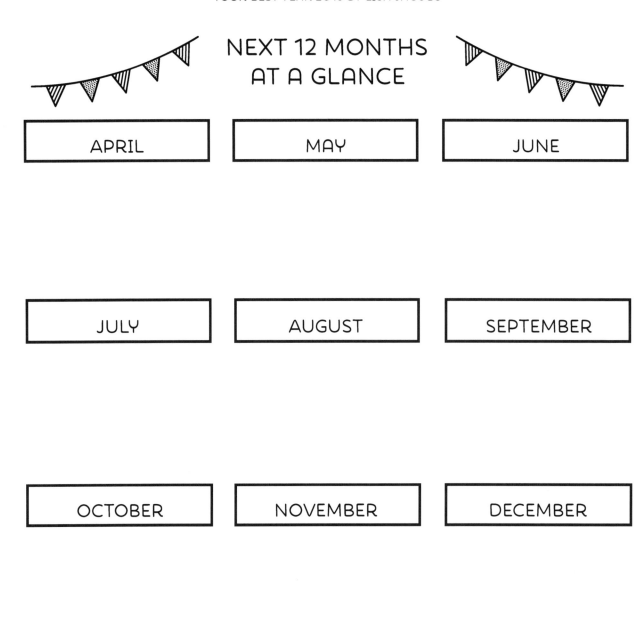

YOUR BEST YEAR 2016 BY LISA JACOBS

 # PROGRESS LOG

WHAT GOALS DO YOU NEED TO COMPLETE IN THE NEXT 3 MONTHS TO STAY ON TRACK WITH YOUR ANNUAL OBJECTIVES?

 ESTIMATE THE TIME EACH PROJECT WILL TAKE & THE AMOUNT OF INCOME YOU CAN EXPECT TO EARN

DUE DATE:

FILL IN THE DISTANCE BETWEEN WHERE YOU ARE NOW AND WHERE YOU WANT TO BE (I.E. ZERO, 25%, 50%, 75%, ETC.):

APRIL 2016

TO-DO	SUNDAY	MONDAY	TUESDAY
☐ ☐ ☐	MARCH 27	28	29
☐ ☐ ☐	3	4	5
☐ ☐ ☐	10	11	12
☐ ☐ ☐ UP NEXT	17	18	19
	24	25	26

YOUR BEST YEAR 2016 BY LISA JACOBS

WEDNESDAY	THURSDAY	FRIDAY	SATURDAY
30	31	1	2
6	7	8	9
13	14	15	16
20	21	22	23
27	28	29	30

APRIL 2016

MONTHLY TO-DO LIST:

☐
☐
☐

☐
☐
☐

☐
☐
☐

☐
☐
☐

PRIORITIES AND PROJECTS:

GOALS TO WORK ON:

FINANCIAL:

SPIRITUAL:

MENTAL:

RELATIONAL:

PHYSICAL:

SPECIAL EVENTS AND APPOINTMENTS TO REMEMBER THIS MONTH:

PROGRESS TRACKER (RECORD PREVIOUS MONTH'S NUMBERS):

FB   PINTEREST   EMAIL   VIEWS   SALES   [   ] [   ] [   ] [   ]

___   ___   ___   ___   ___   ___   ___   ___   ___

APRIL 2016

NEW HABIT TO ADOPT THIS MONTH:	WHAT IS IT TIME TO STOP DOING?

APRIL 3 — APRIL 9
PRIMARY TASKS TO COMPLETE:

NEW HABIT TRACKER:
☐ ☐ ☐ ☐ ☐ ☐ ☐

APRIL 10 — APRIL 16
PRIMARY TASKS TO COMPLETE:

NEW HABIT TRACKER:
☐ ☐ ☐ ☐ ☐ ☐ ☐

APRIL 17 — APRIL 23
PRIMARY TASKS TO COMPLETE:

NEW HABIT TRACKER:
☐ ☐ ☐ ☐ ☐ ☐ ☐

APRIL 24 — APRIL 30
PRIMARY TASKS TO COMPLETE:

NEW HABIT TRACKER:
☐ ☐ ☐ ☐ ☐ ☐ ☐

NOTES:

APRIL 2016 — IN REVIEW

MEMORABLE MOMENTS:

PROJECTS COMPLETED THIS MONTH:

PROJECTS STILL IN THE WORKS:

GOAL PROGRESS:

- FINANCIAL:
- SPIRITUAL:
- MENTAL:
- RELATIONAL:
- PHYSICAL:

MOST IMPORTANT TO ME RIGHT NOW:

WHAT DO I NEED TO IMPROVE?

APRIL 2016 — IN REVIEW

NEW HABIT I WANTED TO ADOPT:

WAS IT A SUCCESS?

IF YES:

NEXT GOOD HABIT TO ADOPT:

IF NO:

WHAT I'LL DO NEXT TO MAKE IT WORK:

WHAT WORKED WELL THIS MONTH:

I.E. POPULAR BLOG POSTS, ENGAGING SOCIAL UPDATES, WAVE OF NEW SUBSCRIBERS

AND WHY?

HOW CAN I REPEAT OR DOUBLE THESE RESULTS?

DID THIS MONTH GET ME CLOSER TO MY ANNUAL OBJECTIVES?

IF YES, HOW WILL I KEEP THAT MOMENTUM?

IF NO, WHAT WILL I DO TO GET BACK ON TRACK?

WHAT OBSTACLE(S) AM I FACING?

WHY IS IT DIFFICULT?

WHAT HAVE I TRIED (SO FAR) TO OVERCOME THE ISSUE(S)?

WHAT CAN I TRY NEXT?

MAY 2016

TO-DO	SUNDAY	MONDAY	TUESDAY
☐ ☐ ☐	1	2	3
☐ ☐ ☐	8	9	10
☐ ☐ ☐	15	16	17
☐ ☐ ☐ UP NEXT	22	23	24
	29	30	31

YOUR BEST YEAR 2016 BY LISA JACOBS

WEDNESDAY	THURSDAY	FRIDAY	SATURDAY
4	5	6	7
11	12	13	14
18	19	20	21
25	26	27	28
JUNE 1	2	3	4

MAY 2016

MONTHLY TO-DO LIST:

☐
☐
☐

☐
☐
☐

☐
☐
☐

☐
☐
☐

PRIORITIES AND PROJECTS:

GOALS TO WORK ON:

💵 FINANCIAL:

⛅ SPIRITUAL:

📚 MENTAL:

👥 RELATIONAL:

⚖ PHYSICAL:

SPECIAL EVENTS AND APPOINTMENTS TO REMEMBER THIS MONTH:

PROGRESS TRACKER (RECORD PREVIOUS MONTH'S NUMBERS):

FB   PINTEREST   EMAIL   VIEWS   SALES   [   ] [   ] [   ] [   ]

___   ___   ___   ___   ___   ___   ___   ___   ___

MAY 2016

NEW HABIT TO ADOPT THIS MONTH:	WHAT IS IT TIME TO STOP DOING?

MAY 1—MAY 7

PRIMARY TASKS TO COMPLETE:

NEW HABIT TRACKER:
☐ ☐ ☐ ☐ ☐ ☐ ☐

MAY 8—MAY 14

PRIMARY TASKS TO COMPLETE:

NEW HABIT TRACKER:
☐ ☐ ☐ ☐ ☐ ☐ ☐

MAY 15—MAY 21

PRIMARY TASKS TO COMPLETE:

NEW HABIT TRACKER:
☐ ☐ ☐ ☐ ☐ ☐ ☐

MAY 22—MAY 28

PRIMARY TASKS TO COMPLETE:

NEW HABIT TRACKER:
☐ ☐ ☐ ☐ ☐ ☐ ☐

MAY 29—JUNE 4

PRIMARY TASKS TO COMPLETE:

NEW HABIT TRACKER:
☐ ☐ ☐ ☐ ☐ ☐ ☐

MAY 2016 — IN REVIEW

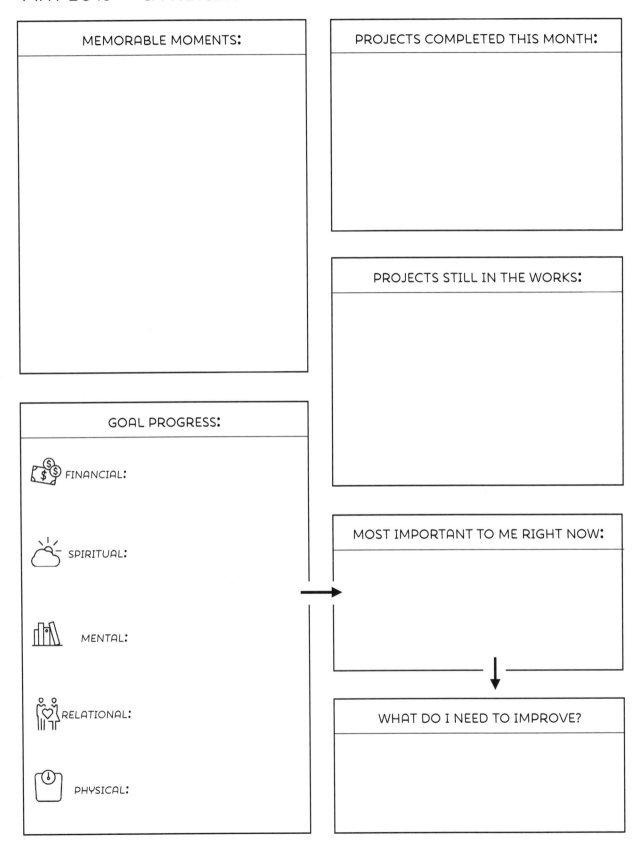

MAY 2016 — IN REVIEW

NEW HABIT I WANTED TO ADOPT:

WHAT WORKED WELL THIS MONTH:

I.E. POPULAR BLOG POSTS, ENGAGING SOCIAL UPDATES, WAVE OF NEW SUBSCRIBERS

WAS IT A SUCCESS?

IF YES:

NEXT GOOD HABIT TO ADOPT:

IF NO:

WHAT I'LL DO NEXT TO MAKE IT WORK:

AND WHY?

HOW CAN I REPEAT OR DOUBLE THESE RESULTS?

DID THIS MONTH GET ME CLOSER TO MY ANNUAL OBJECTIVES?

IF YES, HOW WILL I KEEP THAT MOMENTUM?

IF NO, WHAT WILL I DO TO GET BACK ON TRACK?

WHAT OBSTACLE(S) AM I FACING?

WHY IS IT DIFFICULT?

WHAT HAVE I TRIED (SO FAR) TO OVERCOME THE ISSUE(S)?

WHAT CAN I TRY NEXT?

JUNE 2016

TO-DO	SUNDAY	MONDAY	TUESDAY
☐ ☐ ☐	MAY 29	30	31
☐ ☐ ☐	5	6	7
☐ ☐ ☐	12	13	14
☐ ☐ ☐ UP NEXT	19	20	21
	26	27	28

YOUR BEST YEAR 2016 BY LISA JACOBS

WEDNESDAY	THURSDAY	FRIDAY	SATURDAY
1	2	3	4
8	9	10	11
15	16	17	18
22	23	24	25
29	30	JULY 1	2

JUNE 2016

MONTHLY TO-DO LIST:

☐
☐
☐

☐
☐
☐

☐
☐
☐

☐
☐
☐

PRIORITIES AND PROJECTS:

GOALS TO WORK ON:

FINANCIAL:

SPIRITUAL:

MENTAL:

RELATIONAL:

PHYSICAL:

SPECIAL EVENTS AND APPOINTMENTS TO REMEMBER THIS MONTH:

PROGRESS TRACKER (RECORD PREVIOUS MONTH'S NUMBERS):

FB   PINTEREST   EMAIL   VIEWS   SALES   [   ]   [   ]   [   ]   [   ]

____   _____   _____   _____   _____   _____   _____   _____   _____

JUNE 2016

NEW HABIT TO ADOPT THIS MONTH:	WHAT IS IT TIME TO STOP DOING?

JUNE 5—JUNE 11

PRIMARY TASKS TO COMPLETE:

NEW HABIT TRACKER:
☐ ☐ ☐ ☐ ☐ ☐ ☐

JUNE 12—JUNE 18

PRIMARY TASKS TO COMPLETE:

NEW HABIT TRACKER:
☐ ☐ ☐ ☐ ☐ ☐ ☐

JUNE 19—JUNE 25

PRIMARY TASKS TO COMPLETE:

NEW HABIT TRACKER:
☐ ☐ ☐ ☐ ☐ ☐ ☐

JUNE 26—JULY 2

PRIMARY TASKS TO COMPLETE:

NEW HABIT TRACKER:
☐ ☐ ☐ ☐ ☐ ☐ ☐

NOTES:

JUNE 2016 — IN REVIEW

MEMORABLE MOMENTS:

PROJECTS COMPLETED THIS MONTH:

PROJECTS STILL IN THE WORKS:

GOAL PROGRESS:

FINANCIAL:

SPIRITUAL:

MENTAL:

RELATIONAL:

PHYSICAL:

MOST IMPORTANT TO ME RIGHT NOW:

WHAT DO I NEED TO IMPROVE?

JUNE 2016 — IN REVIEW

NEW HABIT I WANTED TO ADOPT:

WAS IT A SUCCESS?

IF YES:

NEXT GOOD HABIT TO ADOPT:

IF NO:

WHAT I'LL DO NEXT TO MAKE IT WORK:

DID THIS MONTH GET ME CLOSER TO MY ANNUAL OBJECTIVES?

IF YES, HOW WILL I KEEP THAT MOMENTUM?

IF NO, WHAT WILL I DO TO GET BACK ON TRACK?

WHAT WORKED WELL THIS MONTH:

I.E. POPULAR BLOG POSTS, ENGAGING SOCIAL UPDATES, WAVE OF NEW SUBSCRIBERS

AND WHY?

HOW CAN I REPEAT OR DOUBLE THESE RESULTS?

WHAT OBSTACLE(S) AM I FACING?

WHY IS IT DIFFICULT?

WHAT HAVE I TRIED (SO FAR) TO OVERCOME THE ISSUE(S)?

WHAT CAN I TRY NEXT?

MID-YEAR REVIEW

WHAT ARE SOME THINGS YOU COULD BE DOING THAT YOU'VE BEEN AFRAID TO TRY?

HOW CAN YOU STRETCH YOUR COMFORT ZONE?

WHAT IF YOU FAILED? WHAT'S THE WORST-CASE SCENARIO?

WHAT *HUGE* LIFE GOALS WILL YOU WORK TOWARD?

WHAT IF YOU SUCCEEDED? THE BEST-CASE SCENARIO:

IS IT WORTH IT TO TRY?

If I knew I could not fail, I would ...

> "THERE IS FREEDOM WAITING FOR YOU, ON THE BREEZES OF THE SKY, AND YOU ASK, "WHAT IF I FALL?"
>
> OH BUT MY DARLING, WHAT IF YOU FLY? — Erin Hanson

What am I truly craving?

YOUR BIG GOAL:

#1 FAST-FORWARD TO THE TIME IT'S ALREADY COMPLETED. HOW DID YOU MAKE IT HAPPEN? WHAT ACTIONS GOT YOU THERE?

#2 FILL IN THE DISTANCE BETWEEN WHERE YOU ARE NOW AND WHERE YOU WANT TO BE (I.E. ZERO, 25%, 50%, 75%, ETC.):

| STARTING FROM SCRATCH | HALF-WAY POINT | GOAL COMPLETE |

#3 WHAT'S WORKED SO FAR, GETTING YOU CLOSER TO THE GOAL?

#4 BRAINSTORM NEW THINGS YOU MIGHT TRY TO MAKE IT HAPPEN:

#5 ASSIGN A DEADLINE TO GET THIS GOAL 100% COMPLETE:

THE POWER OF 3'S

YOUR BIG GOAL:

WHAT RESULTS DO YOU ANTICIPATE FROM ACHIEVING THIS?

IF YOU STAYED ON THIS COURSE (TRIPLED THESE RESULTS AND KEPT GROWING IN THIS DIRECTION), WHERE WOULD YOU BE IN 3 YEARS?

IF YOU LIKE THOSE RESULTS:

WHAT DO YOU HAVE TO COMPLETE IN THE NEXT 3 MONTHS TO GET STARTED ON THAT?

WHAT DO YOU HAVE TO COMPLETE IN THE NEXT 3 WEEKS TO MAKE PROGRESS?

THE POWER OF 3'S

I'M GOING TO _____

BY _____ YOUR BIG GOAL

DUE DATE

MY DESIRED RESULTS ARE _____

MY CURRENT RESULTS ARE _____

I am grateful for all that I have, accepting of all that I don't, and actively creating all that I want.

BEST-CASE SCENARIO (IF I MEET MY GOAL) _____

WORST-CASE SCENARIO (IF I DON'T) _____

THE POWER OF 3'S

YOUR BIG GOAL:

TO-DO (NEXT 3 MONTHS):

DUE DATE:

TO-DO (NEXT 3 WEEKS):

DUE DATE:

DUE DATE:

DUE DATE:

NEXT SET OF GOALS:

YOUR BEST YEAR 2016 BY LISA JACOBS

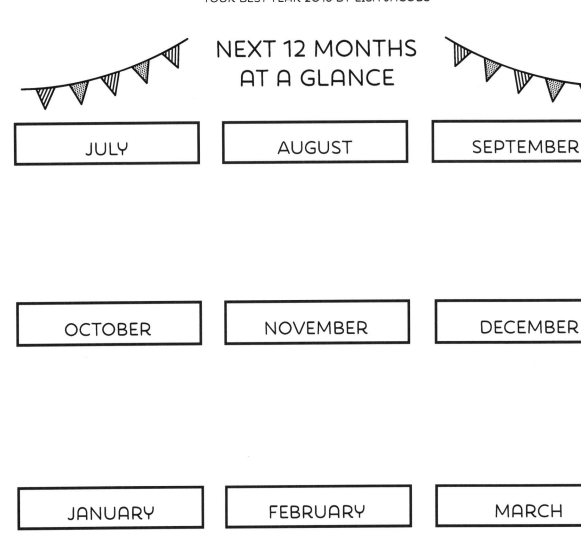

YOUR BEST YEAR 2016 BY LISA JACOBS

 # PROGRESS LOG

WHAT GOALS DO YOU NEED TO COMPLETE IN THE NEXT 3 MONTHS TO STAY ON TRACK WITH YOUR ANNUAL OBJECTIVES?

 ESTIMATE THE TIME EACH PROJECT WILL TAKE & THE AMOUNT OF INCOME YOU CAN EXPECT TO EARN

DUE DATE:

FILL IN THE DISTANCE BETWEEN WHERE YOU ARE NOW AND WHERE YOU WANT TO BE (I.E. ZERO, 25%, 50%, 75%, ETC.):

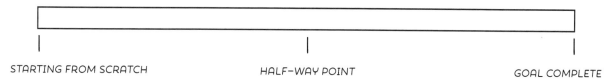

STARTING FROM SCRATCH   HALF-WAY POINT   GOAL COMPLETE

JULY 2016

TO-DO	SUNDAY	MONDAY	TUESDAY
☐ ☐ ☐	JUNE 26	27	28
☐ ☐ ☐	3	4	5
☐ ☐ ☐	10	11	12
☐ ☐ ☐	17	18	19
UP NEXT	24 / 31	25	26

YOUR BEST YEAR 2016 BY LISA JACOBS

WEDNESDAY	THURSDAY	FRIDAY	SATURDAY
29	30	1	2
6	7	8	9
13	14	15	16
20	21	22	23
27	28	29	30

JULY 2016

MONTHLY TO-DO LIST:

☐
☐
☐

☐
☐
☐

☐
☐
☐

☐
☐
☐

PRIORITIES AND PROJECTS:

GOALS TO WORK ON:

FINANCIAL:

SPIRITUAL:

MENTAL:

RELATIONAL:

PHYSICAL:

SPECIAL EVENTS AND APPOINTMENTS TO REMEMBER THIS MONTH:

PROGRESS TRACKER (RECORD PREVIOUS MONTH'S NUMBERS):

FB   PINTEREST   EMAIL   VIEWS   SALES   [   ] [   ] [   ] [   ]

____ _____ _____ _____ _____ _____ _____ _____ _____

JULY 2016

NEW HABIT TO ADOPT THIS MONTH:	WHAT IS IT TIME TO STOP DOING?

JULY 3 — JULY 9
PRIMARY TASKS TO COMPLETE:

NEW HABIT TRACKER:
☐ ☐ ☐ ☐ ☐ ☐ ☐

JULY 10 — JULY 16
PRIMARY TASKS TO COMPLETE:

NEW HABIT TRACKER:
☐ ☐ ☐ ☐ ☐ ☐ ☐

JULY 17 — JULY 23
PRIMARY TASKS TO COMPLETE:

NEW HABIT TRACKER:
☐ ☐ ☐ ☐ ☐ ☐ ☐

JULY 24 — JULY 30
PRIMARY TASKS TO COMPLETE:

NEW HABIT TRACKER:
☐ ☐ ☐ ☐ ☐ ☐ ☐

NOTES:

JULY 2016 — IN REVIEW

MEMORABLE MOMENTS:

PROJECTS COMPLETED THIS MONTH:

PROJECTS STILL IN THE WORKS:

GOAL PROGRESS:

- FINANCIAL:
- SPIRITUAL:
- MENTAL:
- RELATIONAL:
- PHYSICAL:

MOST IMPORTANT TO ME RIGHT NOW:

WHAT DO I NEED TO IMPROVE?

JULY 2016 — IN REVIEW

NEW HABIT I WANTED TO ADOPT:

WAS IT A SUCCESS?

IF YES: **NEXT GOOD HABIT TO ADOPT:**

IF NO: **WHAT I'LL DO NEXT TO MAKE IT WORK:**

DID THIS MONTH GET ME CLOSER TO MY ANNUAL OBJECTIVES?

IF YES, HOW WILL I KEEP THAT MOMENTUM?

IF NO, WHAT WILL I DO TO GET BACK ON TRACK?

WHAT WORKED WELL THIS MONTH:

I.E. POPULAR BLOG POSTS, ENGAGING SOCIAL UPDATES, WAVE OF NEW SUBSCRIBERS

AND WHY?

HOW CAN I REPEAT OR DOUBLE THESE RESULTS?

WHAT OBSTACLE(S) AM I FACING?

WHY IS IT DIFFICULT?

WHAT HAVE I TRIED (SO FAR) TO OVERCOME THE ISSUE(S)?

WHAT CAN I TRY NEXT?

AUGUST 2016

TO-DO	SUNDAY	MONDAY	TUESDAY
☐ ☐ ☐	JULY 31	1	2
☐ ☐ ☐	7	8	9
☐ ☐ ☐	14	15	16
☐ ☐ ☐	21	22	23
UP NEXT	28	29	30

WEDNESDAY	THURSDAY	FRIDAY	SATURDAY
3	4	5	6
10	11	12	13
17	18	19	20
24	25	26	27
31	SEPTEMBER 1	2	3

AUGUST 2016

MONTHLY TO-DO LIST:	PRIORITIES AND PROJECTS:
☐ ☐ ☐ ☐ ☐ ☐ ☐ ☐ ☐ ☐ ☐ ☐	

GOALS TO WORK ON:

FINANCIAL:

SPIRITUAL:

MENTAL:

RELATIONAL:

PHYSICAL:

SPECIAL EVENTS AND APPOINTMENTS TO REMEMBER THIS MONTH:

PROGRESS TRACKER (RECORD PREVIOUS MONTH'S NUMBERS):

FB   PINTEREST   EMAIL   VIEWS   SALES   [   ]   [   ]   [   ]   [   ]

____   ____   ____   ____   ____   ____   ____   ____   ____

AUGUST 2016

NEW HABIT TO ADOPT THIS MONTH:	WHAT IS IT TIME TO STOP DOING?

JULY 31—AUGUST 6

PRIMARY TASKS TO COMPLETE:

NEW HABIT TRACKER:
☐ ☐ ☐ ☐ ☐ ☐ ☐

AUGUST 7—AUGUST 13

PRIMARY TASKS TO COMPLETE:

NEW HABIT TRACKER:
☐ ☐ ☐ ☐ ☐ ☐ ☐

AUGUST 14—AUGUST 20

PRIMARY TASKS TO COMPLETE:

NEW HABIT TRACKER:
☐ ☐ ☐ ☐ ☐ ☐ ☐

AUGUST 21—AUGUST 27

PRIMARY TASKS TO COMPLETE:

NEW HABIT TRACKER:
☐ ☐ ☐ ☐ ☐ ☐ ☐

AUGUST 28—SEPTEMBER 3

PRIMARY TASKS TO COMPLETE:

NEW HABIT TRACKER:
☐ ☐ ☐ ☐ ☐ ☐ ☐

AUGUST 2016 — IN REVIEW

MEMORABLE MOMENTS:

PROJECTS COMPLETED THIS MONTH:

PROJECTS STILL IN THE WORKS:

GOAL PROGRESS:

FINANCIAL:

SPIRITUAL:

MENTAL:

RELATIONAL:

PHYSICAL:

MOST IMPORTANT TO ME RIGHT NOW:

WHAT DO I NEED TO IMPROVE?

AUGUST 2016 — IN REVIEW

NEW HABIT I WANTED TO ADOPT:

WAS IT A SUCCESS?

IF YES:

NEXT GOOD HABIT TO ADOPT:

IF NO:

WHAT I'LL DO NEXT TO MAKE IT WORK:

DID THIS MONTH GET ME CLOSER TO MY ANNUAL OBJECTIVES?

IF YES, HOW WILL I KEEP THAT MOMENTUM?

IF NO, WHAT WILL I DO TO GET BACK ON TRACK?

WHAT WORKED WELL THIS MONTH:

I.E. POPULAR BLOG POSTS, ENGAGING SOCIAL UPDATES, WAVE OF NEW SUBSCRIBERS

AND WHY?

HOW CAN I REPEAT OR DOUBLE THESE RESULTS?

WHAT OBSTACLE(S) AM I FACING?

WHY IS IT DIFFICULT?

WHAT HAVE I TRIED (SO FAR) TO OVERCOME THE ISSUE(S)?

WHAT CAN I TRY NEXT?

SEPTEMBER 2016

TO-DO	SUNDAY	MONDAY	TUESDAY
☐ ☐ ☐	AUGUST 28	29	30
☐ ☐ ☐	4	5	6
☐ ☐ ☐	11	12	13
☐ ☐ ☐	18	19	20
UP NEXT	25	26	27

YOUR BEST YEAR 2016 BY LISA JACOBS

WEDNESDAY	THURSDAY	FRIDAY	SATURDAY
31	1	2	3
7	8	9	10
14	15	16	17
21	22	23	24
28	29	30	OCTOBER 1

SEPTEMBER 2016

MONTHLY TO-DO LIST:

- [ ]
- [ ]
- [ ]

- [ ]
- [ ]
- [ ]

- [ ]
- [ ]
- [ ]

- [ ]
- [ ]
- [ ]

PRIORITIES AND PROJECTS:

GOALS TO WORK ON:

FINANCIAL:

SPIRITUAL:

MENTAL:

RELATIONAL:

PHYSICAL:

SPECIAL EVENTS AND APPOINTMENTS TO REMEMBER THIS MONTH:

PROGRESS TRACKER (RECORD PREVIOUS MONTH'S NUMBERS):

FB   PINTEREST   EMAIL   VIEWS   SALES   [   ]   [   ]   [   ]   [   ]

SEPTEMBER 2016

NEW HABIT TO ADOPT THIS MONTH:	WHAT IS IT TIME TO STOP DOING?

SEPTEMBER 4—SEPTEMBER 10
PRIMARY TASKS TO COMPLETE:

NEW HABIT TRACKER:
☐ ☐ ☐ ☐ ☐ ☐ ☐

SEPTEMBER 11—SEPTEMBER 17
PRIMARY TASKS TO COMPLETE:

NEW HABIT TRACKER:
☐ ☐ ☐ ☐ ☐ ☐ ☐

SEPTEMBER 18—SEPTEMBER 24
PRIMARY TASKS TO COMPLETE:

NEW HABIT TRACKER:
☐ ☐ ☐ ☐ ☐ ☐ ☐

SEPTEMBER 25—OCTOBER 1
PRIMARY TASKS TO COMPLETE:

NEW HABIT TRACKER:
☐ ☐ ☐ ☐ ☐ ☐ ☐

NOTES:

SEPTEMBER 2016 — IN REVIEW

MEMORABLE MOMENTS:

PROJECTS COMPLETED THIS MONTH:

PROJECTS STILL IN THE WORKS:

GOAL PROGRESS:

- FINANCIAL:
- SPIRITUAL:
- MENTAL:
- RELATIONAL:
- PHYSICAL:

MOST IMPORTANT TO ME RIGHT NOW:

WHAT DO I NEED TO IMPROVE?

SEPTEMBER 2016 — IN REVIEW

NEW HABIT I WANTED TO ADOPT:

WAS IT A SUCCESS?

IF YES:

NEXT GOOD HABIT TO ADOPT:

IF NO:

WHAT I'LL DO NEXT TO MAKE IT WORK:

DID THIS MONTH GET ME CLOSER TO MY ANNUAL OBJECTIVES?

IF YES, HOW WILL I KEEP THAT MOMENTUM?

IF NO, WHAT WILL I DO TO GET BACK ON TRACK?

WHAT WORKED WELL THIS MONTH:

I.E. POPULAR BLOG POSTS, ENGAGING SOCIAL UPDATES, WAVE OF NEW SUBSCRIBERS

AND WHY?

HOW CAN I REPEAT OR DOUBLE THESE RESULTS?

WHAT OBSTACLE(S) AM I FACING?

WHY IS IT DIFFICULT?

WHAT HAVE I TRIED (SO FAR) TO OVERCOME THE ISSUE(S)?

WHAT CAN I TRY NEXT?

YOUR BEST YEAR 2016 BY LISA JACOBS

NEXT 12 MONTHS AT A GLANCE

| OCTOBER | NOVEMBER | DECEMBER |

| JANUARY | FEBRUARY | MARCH |

| APRIL | MAY | JUNE |

| JULY | AUGUST | SEPTEMBER |

YOUR BEST YEAR 2016 BY LISA JACOBS

 # PROGRESS LOG

WHAT GOALS DO YOU NEED TO COMPLETE IN THE NEXT 3 MONTHS TO STAY ON TRACK WITH YOUR ANNUAL OBJECTIVES?

 ESTIMATE THE TIME EACH PROJECT WILL TAKE & THE AMOUNT OF INCOME YOU CAN EXPECT TO EARN

DUE DATE:

FILL IN THE DISTANCE BETWEEN WHERE YOU ARE NOW AND WHERE YOU WANT TO BE (I.E. ZERO, 25%, 50%, 75%, ETC.):

STARTING FROM SCRATCH   HALF-WAY POINT   GOAL COMPLETE

OCTOBER 2016

TO-DO	SUNDAY	MONDAY	TUESDAY
☐ ☐ ☐	2	3	4
☐ ☐ ☐	9	10	11
☐ ☐ ☐	16	17	18
☐ ☐ ☐ UP NEXT	23	24	25
	30	31	NOVEMBER 1

YOUR BEST YEAR 2016 BY LISA JACOBS

WEDNESDAY	THURSDAY	FRIDAY	SATURDAY
5	6	7	8
12	13	14	15
19	20	21	22
26	27	28	29
2	3	4	5

OCTOBER 2016

MONTHLY TO-DO LIST:

- ☐
- ☐
- ☐

- ☐
- ☐
- ☐

- ☐
- ☐
- ☐

- ☐
- ☐
- ☐

PRIORITIES AND PROJECTS:

GOALS TO WORK ON:

FINANCIAL:

SPIRITUAL:

MENTAL:

RELATIONAL:

PHYSICAL:

SPECIAL EVENTS AND APPOINTMENTS TO REMEMBER THIS MONTH:

PROGRESS TRACKER (RECORD PREVIOUS MONTH'S NUMBERS):

FB   PINTEREST   EMAIL   VIEWS   SALES   [   ]   [   ]   [   ]   [   ]

____   ____   ____   ____   ____   ____   ____   ____   ____

OCTOBER 2016

NEW HABIT TO ADOPT THIS MONTH:	WHAT IS IT TIME TO STOP DOING?

OCTOBER 2 — OCTOBER 8
PRIMARY TASKS TO COMPLETE:

NEW HABIT TRACKER:
☐ ☐ ☐ ☐ ☐ ☐ ☐

OCTOBER 9 — OCTOBER 15
PRIMARY TASKS TO COMPLETE:

NEW HABIT TRACKER:
☐ ☐ ☐ ☐ ☐ ☐ ☐

OCTOBER 16 — OCTOBER 22
PRIMARY TASKS TO COMPLETE:

NEW HABIT TRACKER:
☐ ☐ ☐ ☐ ☐ ☐ ☐

OCTOBER 23 — OCTOBER 29
PRIMARY TASKS TO COMPLETE:

NEW HABIT TRACKER:
☐ ☐ ☐ ☐ ☐ ☐ ☐

NOTES:

OCTOBER 2016 — IN REVIEW

MEMORABLE MOMENTS:

PROJECTS COMPLETED THIS MONTH:

PROJECTS STILL IN THE WORKS:

GOAL PROGRESS:

- FINANCIAL:
- SPIRITUAL:
- MENTAL:
- RELATIONAL:
- PHYSICAL:

MOST IMPORTANT TO ME RIGHT NOW:

WHAT DO I NEED TO IMPROVE?

OCTOBER 2016 — IN REVIEW

NEW HABIT I WANTED TO ADOPT:

WAS IT A SUCCESS?

IF YES:
NEXT GOOD HABIT TO ADOPT:

IF NO:
WHAT I'LL DO NEXT TO MAKE IT WORK:

WHAT WORKED WELL THIS MONTH:

I.E. POPULAR BLOG POSTS, ENGAGING SOCIAL UPDATES, WAVE OF NEW SUBSCRIBERS

AND WHY?

HOW CAN I REPEAT OR DOUBLE THESE RESULTS?

DID THIS MONTH GET ME CLOSER TO MY ANNUAL OBJECTIVES?

IF YES, HOW WILL I KEEP THAT MOMENTUM?

IF NO, WHAT WILL I DO TO GET BACK ON TRACK?

WHAT OBSTACLE(S) AM I FACING?

WHY IS IT DIFFICULT?

WHAT HAVE I TRIED (SO FAR) TO OVERCOME THE ISSUE(S)?

WHAT CAN I TRY NEXT?

NOVEMBER 2016

TO-DO	SUNDAY	MONDAY	TUESDAY
☐ ☐ ☐	OCTOBER 30	31	1
☐ ☐ ☐	6	7	8
☐ ☐ ☐	13	14	15
☐ ☐ ☐ UP NEXT	20	21	22
	27	28	29

WEDNESDAY	THURSDAY	FRIDAY	SATURDAY
2	3	4	5
9	10	11	12
16	17	18	19
23	24	25	26
30	DECEMBER 1	2	3

NOVEMBER 2016

MONTHLY TO-DO LIST:

☐
☐
☐

☐
☐
☐

☐
☐
☐

☐
☐
☐

PRIORITIES AND PROJECTS:

GOALS TO WORK ON:

FINANCIAL:

SPIRITUAL:

MENTAL:

RELATIONAL:

PHYSICAL:

SPECIAL EVENTS AND APPOINTMENTS TO REMEMBER THIS MONTH:

PROGRESS TRACKER (RECORD PREVIOUS MONTH'S NUMBERS):

FB   PINTEREST   EMAIL   VIEWS   SALES   [   ] [   ] [   ] [   ]

____   _____   _____   _____   _____   _____   _____   _____   _____

NOVEMBER 2016

NEW HABIT TO ADOPT THIS MONTH:	WHAT IS IT TIME TO STOP DOING?

OCTOBER 30 — NOVEMBER 5

PRIMARY TASKS TO COMPLETE:

NEW HABIT TRACKER: ☐ ☐ ☐ ☐ ☐ ☐ ☐

NOVEMBER 6 — NOVEMBER 12

PRIMARY TASKS TO COMPLETE:

NEW HABIT TRACKER: ☐ ☐ ☐ ☐ ☐ ☐ ☐

NOVEMBER 13 — NOVEMBER 19

PRIMARY TASKS TO COMPLETE:

NEW HABIT TRACKER: ☐ ☐ ☐ ☐ ☐ ☐ ☐

NOVEMBER 20 — NOVEMBER 26

PRIMARY TASKS TO COMPLETE:

NEW HABIT TRACKER: ☐ ☐ ☐ ☐ ☐ ☐ ☐

NOVEMBER 27 — DECEMBER 3

PRIMARY TASKS TO COMPLETE:

NEW HABIT TRACKER: ☐ ☐ ☐ ☐ ☐ ☐ ☐

NOVEMBER 2016 — IN REVIEW

MEMORABLE MOMENTS:

PROJECTS COMPLETED THIS MONTH:

PROJECTS STILL IN THE WORKS:

GOAL PROGRESS:

- FINANCIAL:
- SPIRITUAL:
- MENTAL:
- RELATIONAL:
- PHYSICAL:

MOST IMPORTANT TO ME RIGHT NOW:

WHAT DO I NEED TO IMPROVE?

NOVEMBER 2016 — IN REVIEW

NEW HABIT I WANTED TO ADOPT:

WAS IT A SUCCESS?

IF YES:	IF NO:
NEXT GOOD HABIT TO ADOPT:	WHAT I'LL DO NEXT TO MAKE IT WORK:

WHAT WORKED WELL THIS MONTH:
I.E. POPULAR BLOG POSTS, ENGAGING SOCIAL UPDATES, WAVE OF NEW SUBSCRIBERS

AND WHY?

HOW CAN I REPEAT OR DOUBLE THESE RESULTS?

DID THIS MONTH GET ME CLOSER TO MY ANNUAL OBJECTIVES?

IF YES, HOW WILL I KEEP THAT MOMENTUM?

IF NO, WHAT WILL I DO TO GET BACK ON TRACK?

WHAT OBSTACLE(S) AM I FACING?

WHY IS IT DIFFICULT?

WHAT HAVE I TRIED (SO FAR) TO OVERCOME THE ISSUE(S)?

WHAT CAN I TRY NEXT?

DECEMBER 2016

TO-DO	SUNDAY	MONDAY	TUESDAY
☐ ☐ ☐	NOVEMBER 27	28	29
☐ ☐ ☐	4	5	6
☐ ☐ ☐	11	12	13
☐ ☐ ☐	18	19	20
UP NEXT	25	26	27

YOUR BEST YEAR 2016 BY LISA JACOBS

WEDNESDAY	THURSDAY	FRIDAY	SATURDAY
30	1	2	3
7	8	9	10
14	15	16	17
21	22	23	24
28	29	30	31

DECEMBER 2016

MONTHLY TO-DO LIST:

☐
☐
☐

☐
☐
☐

☐
☐
☐

☐
☐
☐

PRIORITIES AND PROJECTS:

GOALS TO WORK ON:

FINANCIAL:

SPIRITUAL:

MENTAL:

RELATIONAL:

PHYSICAL:

SPECIAL EVENTS AND APPOINTMENTS TO REMEMBER THIS MONTH:

PROGRESS TRACKER (RECORD PREVIOUS MONTH'S NUMBERS):

FB   PINTEREST   EMAIL   VIEWS   SALES   [   ]   [   ]   [   ]   [   ]

___   ___   ___   ___   ___   ___   ___   ___   ___

DECEMBER 2016

NEW HABIT TO ADOPT THIS MONTH:	WHAT IS IT TIME TO STOP DOING?

DECEMBER 4 — DECEMBER 10
PRIMARY TASKS TO COMPLETE:

NEW HABIT TRACKER:
☐ ☐ ☐ ☐ ☐ ☐ ☐

DECEMBER 11 — DECEMBER 17
PRIMARY TASKS TO COMPLETE:

NEW HABIT TRACKER:
☐ ☐ ☐ ☐ ☐ ☐ ☐

DECEMBER 18 — DECEMBER 24
PRIMARY TASKS TO COMPLETE:

NEW HABIT TRACKER:
☐ ☐ ☐ ☐ ☐ ☐ ☐

DECEMBER 25 — DECEMBER 31
PRIMARY TASKS TO COMPLETE:

NEW HABIT TRACKER:
☐ ☐ ☐ ☐ ☐ ☐ ☐

NOTES:

DECEMBER 2016 — IN REVIEW

MEMORABLE MOMENTS:

PROJECTS COMPLETED THIS MONTH:

PROJECTS STILL IN THE WORKS:

GOAL PROGRESS:

FINANCIAL:

SPIRITUAL:

MENTAL:

RELATIONAL:

PHYSICAL:

MOST IMPORTANT TO ME RIGHT NOW:

WHAT DO I NEED TO IMPROVE?

DECEMBER 2016 — IN REVIEW

NEW HABIT I WANTED TO ADOPT:

WAS IT A SUCCESS?

IF YES:

NEXT GOOD HABIT TO ADOPT:

IF NO:

WHAT I'LL DO NEXT TO MAKE IT WORK:

DID THIS MONTH GET ME CLOSER TO MY ANNUAL OBJECTIVES?

IF YES, HOW WILL I KEEP THAT MOMENTUM?

IF NO, WHAT WILL I DO TO GET BACK ON TRACK?

WHAT WORKED WELL THIS MONTH:

I.E. POPULAR BLOG POSTS, ENGAGING SOCIAL UPDATES, WAVE OF NEW SUBSCRIBERS

AND WHY?

HOW CAN I REPEAT OR DOUBLE THESE RESULTS?

WHAT OBSTACLE(S) AM I FACING?

WHY IS IT DIFFICULT?

WHAT HAVE I TRIED (SO FAR) TO OVERCOME THE ISSUE(S)?

WHAT CAN I TRY NEXT?

TIPS TO STAY ON TRACK

As human beings, we are creatures of habit and our minds are wired to do the same things over and over again.

For example, I started 2015 determined to double my income, and within two weeks, I caught myself following my old routine — practically guaranteeing I would make the exact same amount I made last year (and the three years before that). I realized early on this year that, in order to double my income, I had to do new and different things!

> INSANITY: DOING THE SAME THING OVER AND OVER AGAIN AND EXPECTING DIFFERENT RESULTS. — *Albert Einstein*

Therefore, I wanted to end this book by giving you a dozen tips that you can implement to keep yourself on track for change

#1 Reduce distractions

Building a business on the internet is distracting enough. You don't need any extra bells, whistles or little red popups, all of which are intentionally designed to interrupt your day!

Therefore, turn off email notifications on your phone. If you have a landline in your home, reserve that for work and emergencies only. Unfollow, remove and/or hide *anyone* that doesn't make your heart sing with inspiration and joy and mutual support. If you are hate-reading, hate-watching or hate-following *anything,* stop that immediately. Unsubscribe and SPAM emails that aren't important. Stop using any social media platforms that don't add to your life, and for the love of everything holy, turn off social notifications and alerts — and never turn those on again!

In other words, put your foot down and say, "NO." Let the world know that the work you do is important and requires your uninterrupted attention.

#2 Schedule regular administration days

I talk to a lot of creative business owners who operate in clutter and chaos. I don't say that to shame anyone, but rather to let you know that if you're operating like that, you are not alone. It happens to us all, at one time or another.

This assignment is for you if …

- Your craft room or home office is a mess
- Your email inbox is cluttered and you struggle to find messages
- New ideas make you feel restless, almost uncomfortable; you desperately want to develop them, but you can't seem to find space in your schedule
- You have so much to do, you don't know where to start
- You find yourself scrolling through hundreds of photos to find the ones you just took
- Your phone storage keeps warning that it's full
- You have unfinished business nagging at you
- Your mind is jumbled; you keep asking, "What did I come in here for?"

An admin day is time you set aside in your work schedule to wear your "secretary hat." Somebody has to clean up the mess around you, organize your clutter and answer your emails! And until you can afford your first assistant, it's going to have to be you.

Schedule your admin day at least one week into the future so that you can create a running to-do list of unfinished business. Have clear goals for the day, such as, an empty inbox, a neat and organized office, a list of inventory, and a revised budget. Then decide how often you need these days throughout the year.

In creative business, it's important to remember and respect all the different hats you need to wear. Your CEO hat (planning, review, decision-making) is as important as your secretary hat (admin, organization and scheduling) and vice versa. In order to run an efficient operation, be sure to take time for these things every month.

#3 Find the right organizational system

I don't mean to be vague, but there isn't a one-size-fits-all organizational system. One of the major differences is whether you prefer to organize digitally or on paper. For me, there's no question! I need paper plans, calendars and project maps, plus loads of empty notebooks. It's the only way for me to bring my new ideas to life.

I've spoken with other creatives who have to have everything digitalized. With today's technology, I can absolutely understand that preference.

The most important part of your organizational system is that you create a way to capture and follow-through on your ideas. The reason digital doesn't work for me is because there's so much going on in so many different places. When I allow myself to take digital notes, they end up on every device I use (phone, iPad, laptop, computer, as well as Pinterest, email, etc.). My digital world is so vast, I easily forget those notes exist!

Inside my paper system, everything has a home. I keep a planner for my blog, a notepad for my upcoming big projects (sectioned for each), a copy of Your Best Year for review, and another day planner for my daily schedule. If something for the blog pops into my mind, I reach for its book (aka its "home" — the only place blog notes are allowed to go), and so on and so forth.

Whatever your system, make sure you designate specific "homes" for the different areas of your work and projects in order to ensure progress.

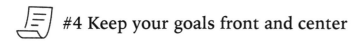 #4 Keep your goals front and center

I feel alive when I'm actively participating and progressing in life, but some years go by when I don't feel I've gotten any closer to my big, dreamy goals. Therefore, I like to keep them front and center (posted on vision boards and in my daily planner), and check-in on my progress towards them every month.

Without a list of goals and regular review, it's easy to get caught up in the daily scramble and chase instant gratification. It's a true challenge to constantly invest in your future and make sacrifices for a better you (tomorrow).

Should I ... exercise or nap? Do that loathsome chore or put it off for another day? Save money toward financial goals or go to Costco? Journal or watch reality TV? Start my next project or click the day away on social media?

These decisions become even more difficult when you don't have reminders of what that "future you" will look and feel like if you make the hard choices today.

 #5 Actively work toward the results you want

All work is not created equal! Results are inevitable: no matter what you do, you're going to get results. Whether they're the results you want or not, well, that's entirely up to you.

Success doesn't just happen to people; you need a deliberate plan and actions you can take to achieve it! Imagine building your dream house without blueprints — you show up every day and let the bricks fall where they may. Do you think you would be perfectly content with the end-result after years of free-form building? No way!

This fly-by-the-seat-of-your-pants mentality has got to go! You must have a clear set of desired results in mind when you show up to do work everyday. Stay focused and on task while constantly challenging yourself to grow.

 #6 Focus on one main goal at a time

This year, set a main goal for each pillar of your life that will get you closer to long-term goals, such as "Pay off all consumer debt" -or- "Lose ten pounds." In order to achieve your main goals successfully, I have some important tips ...

Silence your phone. When you sit down for a movie or presentation, you're asked to turn your phones off to reduce distraction and improve focus. When I'm teaching, I ask my students to give me their undivided attention. I recognize that there are fabulous bloggers and other teachers in the industry, but I liken the overconsumption of everyone's teaching to taking every college-level math class in one semester. All of the different teaching styles, techniques and materials would result in one very confused student!

Ask yourself two important questions ...

1. What *one thing* do I need to learn right now to achieve my goal?
2. Who is the *best* person to teach me that lesson?

The internet is getting noisier by the minute; I'm struggling to keep my own head above it all. I take regular cleanses from social media and use that time to organize my thoughts and notes, remember my own mission (instead of chasing new lessons and bloggers all over Pinterest), and clear my inbox, desk and schedule of busywork.

If you begin to feel overwhelmed and aimless, you might try to "silence your phone" and take a break from all forms of social media as well.

(P.S. If you're thinking to yourself, *There's NO WAY I could leave Facebook for a whole week; I have to check this, post that, etc.,* ... then that's absolute proof that you need to leave Facebook for a week!)

 #7 Appreciate what's abundant

In life and business, it's too easy to focus on what you want and don't have. The best way to shift that feeling of lack and desperation is to bring awareness to what's already abundant in your life.

Want more customers? Enjoy serving your current customer base. Ask yourself:

- How can I treat them like gold?
- What can I do this month to WOW! them?
- How can I use this sale to over-deliver?
- How do I let them know how special they are to me?
- What have other companies done for me that left me feeling appreciated and understood?

You can also spend a month appreciating the material abundance that already surrounds you. Organize your pantry, clean out your closest and drawers, hand wash your car, and spruce up your space in simple and inexpensive ways (like a spray of Febreeze and a vase of fresh flowers).

 ### #8 Identify your symptoms of burnout

Just before burnout hits, I get snarky, overcritical, and addicted to disappointment. I'll have bad dreams that I started smoking again (I quit over a decade ago). Deep in my subconscious, I know I'm relapsing on issues I've already fixed or corrected in my life.

Sometimes, I'll have full-on imaginary arguments in my head with people that are bothering me. Have you ever done this? It's the biggest waste of time and emotion in the universe. I'll snoop on the social media profiles of people I don't like. I'll call a friend who's known to talk about people ... and not change the subject. I'll become the friend known as "the one who likes to talk about people."

> **I MYSELF AM MADE ENTIRELY OF FLAWS, STITCHED TOGETHER WITH GOOD INTENTIONS.**
> — *Augusten Burroughs*

I argue in my head when I want to defend myself against disapproval. I criticize others when I'm lacking self-love and self-respect. My true nature is not negative, sarcastic, or critical. This disposition is a clear signal that I need to recalibrate, and the earlier I catch it, the better.

 ### #9 Learn how to recalibrate your behaviors

Whatever stage you find yourself when you recognize burnout, right your ways at an easy pace. If it's early, start by asking yourself what feelings you're craving and not receiving. A lot of my burnout is caused from feeling a lack of recognition and approval.

Acknowledge the symptoms of burnout, but don't do a sudden u-turn. It's jarring, and will send you into famine which will just continue the cycle. Instead, gently steer yourself back on track.

I always start with some gentle self-talk. When I'm arguing with someone in my head, I'll use Louise Hay's affirmation: "I forgive you for not being what I expected you to be. I forgive you, and I set you free." If it continues, I'll firmly say to the imaginary person I'm arguing with: "You don't belong here." With that, I make a conscious choice to come back to the present moment and appreciate the here and now.

Since I know these arguments come from a place of wanting respect and approval, I'll replace the negative thought process with some positive affirmations. "I love and approve of myself" works wonders for me. Without knowing I'm intentionally repeating that saying, my family has commented on a noticeable difference in my demeanor when I replace mindless rumination with meaningful and positive affirmations.

I'll also seek out a new form of entertainment at this stage. I wasn't kidding when I said I'd prefer extremes to boredom. I love to be entertained in the evening, and there's a noticeable shift in my overall happiness when I've got nothing fun to do with my few spare hours before bed.

I've learned that I need a good fiction read in my life, and it's for just those occasions. Knowing I have a story to get lost in makes me a happier human being overall, and I think reading is such a clean and recharging form of entertainment.

 #10 Leave some business on the table

Whaaaaat? Yes, you heard me correctly! Believe it or not, you don't want every customer.

Before I opened my membership program, a reader told me she was excited and asked how much The Luminaries Club was going to cost. I hadn't announced the price yet but I knew her from another project, so I told her it was going to start at 34 dollars per month. She said she probably wouldn't join because she was a "cheapskate."

I appreciated her honesty. Moreover, I appreciated the chance to tell her that the club I built probably isn't for her. I pour everything I've got into it. I'm invested in my client's success, and I work hard for them. I'm a fiercely loyal employee!

When people want "cheap," we're not a good professional fit, and that's okay. If they don't want to invest in their business, I certainly don't want to either! In the last four years, I've hired graphic designers, virtual assistants, private coaches, copywriters and mentors to help take my business to the next level. To me, it's the natural order of things, and I love having a team I can count on.

The fact of the matter is: cheapskates are nobody's ideal customer. They feel entitled to the results, but they don't want to make the investment. And because they're so unwilling to invest, they're constantly disappointed with their situation and eager to complain.

 #11 **Develop a daily practice**

A routine that offers a schedule to follow is one of the most important things you can create for yourself. It not only helps you build new patterns and habits, it also saves vast amounts of mental energy essential for the critical and creative thinking you'll need throughout the day.

No business is complete without the simple things: a solid daily practice, a plan for long-term growth, and a clearing of unfinished work and nagging obligations.

 #12 **Take it one day at a time**

I mentioned this before, and it bears repeating. Don't let a lazy, overindulgent weekend spoil all of your efforts. If you slip off course, it only takes one good decision to get you right back on track. With bigger goals (that take longer to achieve), it's better to work every day toward long-term transformation rather than try to adhere to rigid deadlines with a "succeed or fail" mindset.

For example, if your goal is to become debt-free by a certain deadline, and you miss it, you're more likely to carry the debt longer. However, if your goal is to change your life by becoming debt-free (and keep it that way), you're more likely to see that intention as a new way of life rather than a gamble that you may win or lose.

Your daily routine will help you stay (and get back) on track. Without it, you're more likely to return to outworn patterns and old habits. Set a work schedule, a workout schedule, and a chore schedule. And then challenge yourself to follow it for just one day. Then another. And then a week!

A day planner proves to be a very useful tool so that you can write down what you'd like to accomplish in advance, and cross it off when it's complete.

VALUABLE RESOURCES

The Luminaries Club[5] — If you found this book useful, you will absolutely love my membership program. It is my favorite way to work with creatives, and it's also the most affordable coaching I offer.

Inside the club, you'll get unlimited access to all of my current programs, courses, and guides. I regularly release training classes and material, and I personally keep in touch with Luminaries via our private network.

I invite you to join our club of like-minded, successful creatives and continue your business planning and education, so that I may help you reach, connect with, and sell to your ideal customers.

As a special bonus for Your Best Year readers, I've set up a $20 credit that can either be applied to the monthly fee or annual payment. To redeem, use promo code: **YBY2016** — I hope to welcome you there soon!

---

[5] HTTP://WWW.MARKETYOURCREATIVITY.COM/LUMINARIES-CLUB/

Inbox Pause[6] — I have this on my main work account (gmail) to reduce the temptation to constantly check email. Inbox Pause only allows your email to deliver at set times per day. You can set it as frequently (every hour) or as rarely (once or twice a day) as you like.

I love this for workdays as it has greatly reduced my clicking addiction!

Browser extensions — I switched to Google's Chrome browser this year because one of my main working sites was not compatible with Safari (my previous browser). Since the switch, I've found a few of Chrome's extensions invaluable to my creative business.

In case I'm speaking a foreign language to you, your different web browsers (Chrome, Safari, Firefox) are all coming out with "extensions" — you might have noticed Pinterest push for you to add their extension to your browser; that was my first exposure to it. Now I have an entire collection.

Here are the extensions I just can't live without:

Alexa[7] — Alexa is a website ranking tool. You install it to your browser window, and when you visit a website, you click the extension button and it will show you exactly how popular the site is (or isn't).

This is extremely useful for people with their own domain, as you can watch what helps your ranking (global and domestic) and what hurts it. I also love it for determining whether online business owners are the real deal ("I get hundreds of emails every single day, make six figures, and sell out of everything I make!") versus just another joker making false internet claims.

If you're a blogger, this extension is also a great way to determine if guest posting for others will be worth your time and efforts or not.

---

[6] HTTP://INBOXPAUSE.COM/

[7] HTTP://WWW.ALEXA.COM/TOOLBAR?BROWSER=CHROME

Color Picker[8] — I absolutely love this extension as I've done a lot of my own design this year. Color picker puts a little dropper on your browser bar, and you can pull colors from any place on the internet. It then keeps your picked colors and gives you the design code (i.e., #0e1d3a for navy blue). You can then plug that number into any graphic creator for the perfect match!

Stay Focusd[9] — This extension is a productivity tool that lets you limit or ban websites from your computer for a set amount of time. For example, I might only allow myself 10 minutes on Facebook, and then Stay Focused will ban it and pull up a screen that says: "Shouldn't you be working?" And my answer to that question is always: "Why yes, I should be!"

It also has a "nuclear option." This will completely block a site that you use for a set amount of hours (which you enter and adjust yourself). I frequently nuke Twitter; it's just not an effective use of my time.

Alternative: If you don't need the internet while you work, Strict Workflow[10] might be better for reducing distraction. It won't allow you to visit any site while your work timer is on, but this doesn't work for me because I often need to reference stats, research and content from my blog when I write.

In closing, I applaud your commitment to building your own creative business. Thank you so much for having the courage to chase your dreams. Thank you for creating your beautiful art. Thank you for making this world come more alive because you're in it. I commend you for showing up to all of that, every day.

> BECAUSE TO FOLLOW A CALLING REQUIRES WORK. IT'S HARD. IT HURTS. IT DEMANDS ENTERING THE PAIN-ZONE OF EFFORT, RISKS, AND EXPOSURE.
> — *Steven Pressfield*

If you should need me, find me in my zone — talking shop and writing away — at www.marketyourcreativity.com. Here's to your best year yet!

---

[8] http://www.colorzilla.com/

[9] https://chrome.google.com/webstore/detail/stayfocusd/laankejkbhbdhmipfmgcngdelahlfoji?hl=en

[10] https://chrome.google.com/webstore/detail/strict-workflow/cgmnfnmlficgeijcalkgnnkigkefkbhd?hl=en

Printed in Great Britain
by Amazon.co.uk, Ltd.,
Marston Gate.